Adolphe de Chambrun

The Executive Power in the United States

A Study of Constitutional Law

Adolphe de Chambrun

The Executive Power in the United States
A Study of Constitutional Law

ISBN/EAN: 9783337031671

Printed in Europe, USA, Canada, Australia, Japan

Cover: Foto ©Suzi / pixelio.de

More available books at **www.hansebooks.com**

THE

EXECUTIVE POWER

IN THE

UNITED STATES:

A STUDY OF

CONSTITUTIONAL LAW.

BY

ADOLPHE DE CHAMBRUN.

TRANSLATED FROM THE ORIGINAL FRENCH

BY

MRS. MADELEINE VINTON DAHLGREN.

Votes cannot INSURE equal rights to all.

Taxes are, or should be, paid to support the institutions of society—not for the purpose of placing certain men *in office.*

LANCASTER, PA.
INQUIRER PRINTING AND PUBLISHING COMPANY.
1874.

PREFACE.

ERRATA.

Preface, p. 1, line 14, for " have" read " prove ;" line 15, for " experiments" read " experiment."

Chapter II., page 52, line 8, for " Russa" read " Russia."

P. 122, line 9, for " repell" read " repel."

P. 127, line 12, interpolate *the* between " executive" and " preponderating."

P. 176, line 14, for *ca ira* read *ça ira*.

P. 7, Opinions of the Press, line 30, for "open" read " pen."

This volume offers a new and striking illustration of the fact that many of the characteristics and tendencies of a nation are better understood and appreciated by foreigners than by native citizens. The foreign student has an advantage in the stand-point from which he makes his observation. He studies the institutions from a distance, and is able to measure them by other standards with less bias, perhaps, than those whose opinions have become a part of the public thought of

(iii)

PREFACE.

It will be generally conceded that the most profound and searching discussion of the democratic principle and of the character and tendencies of the Government of the United States, which has appeared in modern times, is that of De Tocqueville. Many of his chapters sound like prophecy when read in the light of recent events. The monograph of the Marquis De Chambrun on the Executive Power of the United States is a worthy continuation of De Tocqueville's discussion. It is the first of a series of four volumes, which the author proposes to publish, on the several departments and functions of our Government. Should the series be completed with the thoroughness and ability manifested in this volume, it will have a repertory of the most valuable political results of our republican experiments.

This volume offers a new and striking illustration of the fact that many of the characteristics and tendencies of a nation are better understood and appreciated by foreigners than by native citizens. The foreign student has an advantage in the stand-point from which he makes his observation. He studies the institutions from a distance, and is able to measure them by other standards with less bias, perhaps, than those whose opinions have become a part of the public thought of the country whose institutions they discuss. This truth has frequently been exemplified in the criticism of National literature.

It is worthy of remark that the efforts to recover the fame of Shakespeare from the oblivion into which it had fallen at the end of the 17th century was made by men who did not speak the language of Shakespeare. It was to Voltaire, Gœthe and Schlegel, that the world was chiefly indebted for the Shakespearian revival.

This volume of the Executive Power of the United States is another striking illustration of the same truth, applied to political philosophy. While the author is an ardent supporter of republican government, he has evidently escaped the error that so many writers have fallen into—that of believing that our forms can be safely adopted by all nations.

Throughout the volume the author keeps two objects constantly in view, viz.: To study our institutions in relation to the traditions, spirit and tendencies of our own people; and to ascertain what features of our institutions are adapted to the tradition and spirit of European nations. This comparative study will be most interesting to the student of political philosophy.

In discussing the relation of the office of the Vice-President to our system, the author notices the fact, which I think has not been elsewhere discussed, that the office of Vice-President, while it is valuable for the purposes of an election—the candidate being usually selected with a view to supplementing the opinions of the candidate for the Presidency—yet this very fact makes the Vice-President an inharmonious element for purposes of administration. The author traces to this cause the fact that whenever our Vice-President has become President, his administration has not been satisfactory to the country. On the whole, the author doubts the value of the office of Vice-President, and says that our example in this particular should not be followed elsewhere.

After giving a masterly analysis of the constitutional power of the Executive, the author discusses the advantages and disadvantages of the frequent changes in the Presidency by popular elections, and concludes that the instability of the office is in the interest of liberty.

The fourth chapter contains a very clear and interesting sketch of the conflicts that have occurred from time to time between the Executive and the Legislative departments, and concludes with the declaration that on the whole "The prerogatives of the President are to-day nearly what they were in the time of Washington, though they have been rather increased than diminished."

The chapters of this work which will be of most interest to the people of the United States are those in which the author discusses the effects of the late civil war upon our system of government. It is hardly possible for those who have been actors in the Executive, Legislative, or Judicial Departments of the Government to realize the changes which recent events have produced. The author of these chapters has rendered a great service to every thoughtful American, in setting forth with remarkable clearness and force the changes which recent events have wrought.

Starting from the antagonistic views of Hamilton and Jefferson, the one insisting upon a strong central Government—the other upon the preponderance of power in the people and the States—the author traces clearly the influence of those two forces upon all our subsequent history, and predicts that the safety of our system depends upon the equilibrium of these two forces. He concludes this portion of his discussion by saying that " so long as political activity in the States remains undiminished, and the existing division of sovereignty between them and the national government continues, the equilibrium will not be deranged. The Executive authority cannot imperil the Constitution, unless the local autonomies first disappear or become sensibly weakened."

The author has been peculiarly fortunate in his selection of the translator.   His thought has been faithfully rendered into clear and elegant English ; and the work has been done with so much grace that the reader discovers nothing in the style to indicate that it is a translation.

JAMES A. GARFIELD.

WASHINGTON, MARCH 16, 1874.

NOTICE.

SINCE 1776, when the thirteen colonies of North America proclaimed their Declaration of Independence and defined the principles of modern democracy, we have beheld the decay or transformation of feudalism almost everywhere in Europe.

In view of such a state of things, the historian and the statesman, without yielding to the promptings of the heart, or to the flights of the imagination, should calmly observe and classify facts and strive to deduce therefrom the laws that reg-. ulate the political progress of nations.

If, then, we inquire what forms of government democratic nations may substitute for those of the past, we are naturally led to study the organization of the American republic. In pursuing such researches, the most suitable order to follow is that invariably adopted by the Federal Constitution, as well as the constitutions of the thirty-seven States of the Union. Attention should be given first to the national sovereignty and the supreme power of the people; and then to the organization of the legislative, the executive and the judicial branches of the government.

It has appeared to me, however, that such a work, for which much material has been slowly gathered, might properly be divided into four almost entirely distinct parts, and each of them be treated in a separate publication. Acting upon that impression, I have not hesitated to issue in the first place this *monograph* on The Executive Power.

The question which it is proposed to examine in the book now submitted to the public is this: How have a democratic people succeeded in organizing an executive power which was, up to a certain point, to take the place elsewhere occupied by historic royalty, or by that constitutional monarchy of which England has produced the model ?

Inasmuch as the knowledge I have acquired of the Constitution of the United States has been principally gained in the course of an intimate association with some eminent men, I desire to mention Senator Charles Sumner, Mr. Caleb Cushing and Senator Schurz as those to whom I am the most indebted. The literary world of Europe will soon be in possession of the complete works of Mr. Sumner. It will then be able to appreciate the vast learning of this statesman, to understand his superior nature, and to catch at least the faint echo of those austere and eloquent utterances, which I have never heard without being reminded of what the cotemporaries of our Royer-Collard have told us of him.

After Mr. Sumner, I have named that jurisconsult who has never separated the cultivation of letters from the study of law, and whose attention has been alternately directed to the most diverse branches of human knowledge ; after having filled the highest political positions to which an American may aspire, he has retired from the arena of political parties, reserving to himself only the right of judging their acts.

Finally, I have spoken of Senator Schurz, a German, naturalized in the United States; he has applied to the study of the institutions of the country, to which he has forever promised allegiance, the rigorous methods of European criticism, and thus imparted those enlarged views and that political philosophy which give to his speeches and writings a lasting value.

I take the liberty to place, under the protection of these distinguished men, the work of which I offer now to the public the first portion.[1]

WASHINGTON, FEBRUARY 18, 1873.

[1] The works to which I refer are always quoted, so as to be as accessible as possible to the European reader. Thus, for example, when I have found the decisions of the Supreme Court reprinted in books which could be easily procured, I have cited the latter in preference to the reports of that tribunal.

TABLE OF CONTENTS.

(ix)

INTRODUCTION.

THE organization of the Executive Power in a republic offers the greatest difficulties. It should have vigor and capacity to meet the necessities of the government without proving an obstacle to the development of the liberties of the country.

There would seem to be, at first, almost a contradiction between propositions so dissimilar, and yet, if they cannot be harmonized, the republic will either be lost in anarchy or replaced by military despotism.

From the moment when the American people decided that they would thenceforth live under democratic and republican institutions, questions regarding the constitution of the Executive Power were naturally presented for their consideration. The most opposite opinions on the subject were at once expressed, traces of which will be found in the debates which took place in the Constitutional Convention of Philadelphia.[1]

Alexander Hamilton's plan provided for the vesting of the supreme executive authority in a Governor, to be chosen by electoral colleges, and to serve during good behavior, his authorities and functions to be as follows: To have a negative on all laws about to be passed, and the execution of all laws passed; to have the direction of war, when authorized or begun; to

---

[1] The convention of 1787 deliberated with closed doors. James Madison, one of its members, drew up a summary of these debates, which has been published under the title of "The Madison Papers."

have, with the advice and approbation of the Senate, the power of making all treaties; to have the sole appointment of the heads or chief officers of the departments of finance, war and foreign affairs; to have the nomination of all other officers (ambassadors to foreign nations included), subject to the approbation or rejection of the Senate; to have the power of pardoning all offenses, except treason, which he could not pardon without the approbation of the Senate. "On the death, resignation or removal of the Governor, his authorities shall be exercised by the president of the Senate until a successor be appointed." [1]

At the time that Hamilton thus proposed to create a strong power, another member of the convention, Roger Sherman, maintained, on the contrary, that the executive magistrate should be simply the agent of the legislature. Others went still further by even denying the principle of unity, and insisting that the Executive Power could not be confided to one man without danger to liberty.

After elaborate discussions, the convention finally agreed and adopted a compromise. It, in the first place, recognized the principle of unity, and committed the Executive Power to a single magistrate, who was to be elected for four years. In the second place, that power was constituted one of the three "co-ordinate and independent" branches of the government, and clothed with considerable prerogatives. It was finally decided that no constitutional council should be assigned the President, but that he should be the acting

1 The Madison Papers, Vol. II., p. 890 *et seq.*

and responsible head of the federal administration. These principles are all set forth in the Constitution, and for more than eighty years have been of constant application.

It cannot be said that the members of the convention were entirely satisfied with their work. When defending it before the Virginia Convention, James Madison frankly avowed that the organization of the Executive Power was attended with peculiar difficulties, and it is worthy of remark that he simply asserted that the convention had acted for the best.

Notwithstanding the doubts he expressed on the subject, that Power has remained such as it was conceived by the convention. It has met the wants of a free people, and been able to resist formidable dangers.

Thus, to explain why this has been so, is the principal aim of the present volume.

However, it would not answer for other nations who are inclined to adopt " a republican form of government," to believe that they can copy the Federal Constitution and solve, as the Americans have done, the problems regarding the powers and prerogatives of the President. Republican institutions in the United States were founded in historic right. The thirteen colonies lived under democratic laws long before their separation from the mother country. At the same time the inhabitants of English birth brought with them all the customs of Anglo-Saxon liberty.

They had, gradually, established in the new world a close alliance between democracy and free institutions, 'which eventually gave rise to the republic. It had existed in the national manners before it received its definitive form; and those who proclaimed it only recognized and gave effect to a long established state of things.

This is true to such an extent that it is difficult to find in the writings of that day a satisfactory explanation of the manner of adopting the "republican form of government" in the United States. Some years before his death Thomas Jefferson carefully prepared a memoir, wherein he recounts the part that he had taken in the struggle of the thirteen colonies, in the Declaration of Independence, and in the succeeding events. The word republic is not once mentioned in this work.

The convention was not appointed to choose between different forms of government; its mission was restricted to the formation of such institutions as were best adapted to the country. Thus the republic has been able to maintain itself in the United States, because it represents public sentiment and national traditions. It performs there, in some respects, a similar part to that which has been elsewhere enacted by monarchies or historical aristocracies.

In the second place the convention was called upon to find the best possible compromise between the local autonomies, which had for a long time existed, and the central government it was about to create. It divided the sovereignty then between the states and the federal government, and conferred upon the latter, by the consent of the people to whom it owed its existence, only certain limited powers specifically enumerated in the Constitution.

Out of this arose a division of powers which cannot elsewhere be imitated.

In short, the United States did not from the beginning propose to follow in the footsteps of other nations. They desired to "form a government capable of extending to its citizens all the blessings of civil and religious liberty, capable of making them happy at home. This, and not conquests or superiority, is the great object of republican systems." "If they are sufficiently active and energetic," said one of their distinguished statesmen, "to rescue us from contempt and preserve our domestic happiness and security, it is all that we can expect from them."[1]

In other words, the American Republic enjoys the inestimable advantages which result as well from a constant national tradition as from a perfectly logical division of powers between vigorous autonomies and the central institutions. It should, therefore, seek its perpetuity in the peaceful development of its own vital forces, and maintain, as far as practicable, an isolated position among other nations.

The people of other countries, who are considering the expediency of establishing American institutions, should only do so with the most guarded caution. The object of the following expositions is, however, merely to explain how the Executive Power is organized in the United States. The European reader must decide to what extent the forms of American institutions can be introduced in countries having a monarchical past,

1 The Madison Papers, Vol. II., p. 95 *et. seq.;* speech of Mr. Pinckney.

where the system of centralization has thrust its roots far and deep, and where exterior action has become a necessary condition of national life.

But it is impossible to enter upon the study of problems so complicated as those which, even in the United States, arise out of the organization of the Executive Power, without at once recurring in thought to M. de Tocqueville, and feeling serious apprehension at the boldness of treating a subject upon which he has shed a flood of light. "Democracy in America" can neither be equaled nor repeated. Its appearance inaugurated a new epoch in political science, and it was at once classed among that small number of writings which have advanced this very important branch of human knowledge. However, since the publication of this masterly work, events of the gravest import have occurred in the United States. The Federal Constitution has been subjected to trials, foreseen indeed by M. de Tocqueville, but the consequences of which his premature death prevented him from measuring. Learned researches and numerous publications have thrown new light upon the authority of the national government over the several States and the people. There is, perhaps, an advantage in exhibiting the changes that have taken place, and in analyzing the views recently expressed by authors and statesmen, whose opinions are of acknowledged authority. Nevertheless it may be safely asserted, that the literature relating to America which has appeared during the past thirty years has not deprived the "Democracy" of the exceptional place it had acquired. It always recalls

those chapters, in which Montesquieu made known to
France the liberty which is the birthright of Englishmen, and described the structure and inner working
of their celebrated constitution. Other writers have succeeded the author of *"L'esprit des lois."* They have
discussed the same questions; they have thoroughly
examined the prerogatives of the crown, the powers
of each house of Parliament and the relations which
exist between them; they have traced and explained
the influence of the historic causes which have developed and perfected those noble institutions. Blackstone, Brougham, and others in England; Fishel, and
especially Gneist, in Germany, have exhausted the subject, and yet over all their works still towers the
genius of Montesquieu, " who abridged all, because he
had seen all."

2

THE EXECUTIVE POWER

IN

THE UNITED STATES.

CHAPTER I.

ELECTION OF PRESIDENT AND VICE-PRESIDENT.

THE members of the convention, in considering the questions relative to the Executive Power, had to determine whether the chief magistrate should be directly elected by the people, or be designated by the legislative power. Each system had its partisans. Finally, a compromise was adopted. It was decided that "each State shall appoint, in such manner as the inhabitants thereof may direct, a number of electors equal to the whole number of Senators and Representatives to which the State may be entitled.........that the electors shall meet in their respective States and vote by ballot for President and Vice-president." The Constitution adds, "the votes shall be forwarded to the President of the Senate at the seat of government, and the person having the greatest number of votes shall be the President, if such number be a majority of the whole number of electors appointed, and if there be more than one who have such majority, and have an equal number of votes, then the House of Representatives shall immediately choose by ballot one of them for President; and if no person have a majority, then from the five highest on the list the said House shall in like manner choose the President."[1]   If then the convention refused to confide directly to the people the election of the President, neither did it invest the legislative as-semblies with so important a right.   Hamilton has explained, in the "Federalist," the motives which led to the adoption of this compromise.[2]

"Nothing," said he, "was more to be desired than that every practicable obstacle should be opposed to cabal, intrigue and corruption.   These most deadly adversaries of republican government might naturally have been expected to make their approaches from more than one quarter, but chiefly from the desire in foreign powers to gain an improper ascendant in our councils.............But the convention has guarded against all danger of this sort with the most provident and judicious

---

1 See Constitution of the United States.

2 The best commentary on the Constitution of the United States is to be found in the "Federalist." It was written by Alexander Hamilton, James Madison and John Jay. The first two were members of the Philadelphia Convention. This admirable publi-cation supplies, to some extent, the void in American political literature occasioned by the failure to record the full debates of that body.

attention. They have not made the appointment
of the President to depend on any pre-existing
bodies of men, who might be tampered with beforehand to prostitute their votes; but they have
referred it in the first instance to an immediate act
of the people of America, to be exerted in the
choice of persons for the temporary and sole purpose of making the appointment; and they have
excluded from eligibility to this trust all those who
from situation might be suspected of too great devotion to the President in office. No Senator, Representative or other person holding a place of trust
or profit under the United States can be of the
numbers of the electors. Thus, without corrupting
the body of the people, the immediate agents in
the election will at least enter upon the task free
from any sinister bias. Their transient existence
and their detached situation, already taken notice
of, afford a satisfactory prospect of their continuing
so to the conclusion of it. The business of corruption, when it is to embrace so considerable a number of men, requires time as well as means. Nor
would it be found easy suddenly to embark them,
dispersed as they would be over thirteen States, in
any combinations founded upon motives which,
though they could not properly be denominated
corrupt, might yet be of a nature to mislead them
from their duties." It was essential, and this was
no less important, that the Executive Power should

depend on the people alone during the exercise of
its functions. "He might otherwise be tempted to
sacrifice his duty to his complaisance for those
whose favor was necessary to the duration of his
official consequence. This advantage will also be
secured by making his re-election to depend on a
special body of representatives deputed by the
society for the single purpose of making the important choice."[1]

It is noticeable that Hamilton, who exposes so
forcibly the grave objections to the election of the
President by legislative assemblies, is much less
explicit when he criticises the system of direct
election by the people. Yet this subject was several times under discussion in the convention,
but the members set it aside for various reasons,
which were, notwithstanding, very unsatisfactory.
They feared that the people were not sufficiently
enlightened to make an intelligent choice of the
executive chief; they also apprehended difficulties
as to the manner of execution

However that may be, the election of the President by the National Legislature having been
rejected, and the direct election by the people
having shared the same fate, there remained no
alternative but to organize, in the most satisfactory
manner, the electoral colleges.

But the resulting consequences were far from

---

[1] The "Federalist," pp. 474-475. Edition of Henry B. Dawson.

justifying the expectation of the convention. It soon became evident that the electoral colleges had no will of their own, and that their members were pledged in advance to cast their votes for a candidate designated by the party to which they themselves owed their election. In this particular the system proved a failure.

But according to the Constitution, under certain contingencies, a second election could be held. This case speedily occurring, it was found that here, also, experience was far from vindicating theory. As we have just seen, if there was no choice, either because no one candidate received an absolute majority, or because several of them obtained an equal number of votes, then, by a provision of the Constitution, the House of Representatives must, in its turn, resolve itself, if the expression may be allowed, into an electoral college. In that case it would then choose the President from among the five persons who had the greatest number of votes; or, yet again, if two candidates had the same majority it would decide between them.

Nor was there then a separate vote for President and Vice-president; the ballots did not designate the office that the persons in whose favor they were given were to fill. According to this provision, the person who received the greatest number of votes, if such number was equal to a majority of the whole number of electors appointed, became President, and the one who, having the next greatest number of votes, providing it 'was a majority, was elected Vice-president. But from the outset the people made a distinction between these two offices, and, in fact, cast their votes for *President* and for *Vice-president.* However, according to the letter of the Constitution, the House of Representatives might decline accepting the result of the popular election, and it was authorized to select for the presidential office the person whom the people had intended to choose for Vice-president. But here also all the constitutional combinations were of no avail. The will of the people proved stronger than that of the Legislature. This was shown in the election of 1801.

This was the first which had devolved upon the House of Representatives. Mr. Jefferson and Mr. Burr had an absolute majority in the electoral colleges. Each of them received seventy-five votes. Although the people had only nominated Mr. Burr as Vice-president, the House could have elected him President. The delegations of the States where the Federalists prevailed proposed to accomplish this result. However, the most distinguished of them—Hamilton—rose under these circumstances superior to party considerations. The people's choice was Jefferson, and Hamilton made an effort to have this verdict accepted as definitive. Thanks,

at least in a measure to his influence, the Demo-
/cratic principle prevailed. After this animated
contest, which lasted seven days and seven nights,
the Constitution was amended by providing that
the electors shall meet in their respective States,[1]
and vote by ballot for President and Vice-president
.........they shall make distinct lists of all persons
voted for as President, and of all persons voted for
as Vice-president, and of the number of votes for
each, which lists they shall sign and certify, and
transmit, sealed, to the seat of the government of
the United States, directed to the president of the
Senate. The president of the Senate shall, in the
presence of the Senate and House of Representatives, open all the certificates, and the votes shall
then be counted; the person having the greatest
number of votes for President shall be the President
.........and if no person have a majority, then from
the two highest numbers, not exceeding three of
those voted for as President on the list, the House
of Representatives shall choose immediately by ballot the President; but in choosing the President,
the votes shall be taken by States, the representation from each State having one vote."........How-
ever, " in choosing, the President," adds the amend-

1 See The Political Parties in the United States, by Martin Van
Buren. This work, written by a former President of the United
States, cannot be read too often. He has shown much impartiality
in his political views, and furnished very varied, and, in general,
very reliable, information.

ment, "the votes shall be counted by States, and each State shall have a vote.[1]

These constitutional provisions were applied for the first time in 1824. "General Jackson, Mr. John Quincy Adams and Mr. William H. Crawford were the three candidates for the presidency who received the highest number of votes—99, 84, 41; and in this case a second struggle took place between the theory of the Constitution and the Democratic principle, and with eventual defeat to the opposers of that principle, though temporarily successful. Mr. Adams was elected, though General Jackson was the choice of the people..........The election of Mr. Adams was perfectly constitutional, and as such fully submitted to by the people.........All the representatives who voted against the will of their constituents lost their favor, and disappeared from public life. The representation in the House of Representatives was largely changed at the first general election, and presented a full opposition to the new President. Mr. Adams himself was injured by it, and at the ensuing presidential election was beaten by General Jackson more than two to one—178 to 83."[2]

Thus the electoral colleges have never had the right of expressing a free opinion, and, on the other hand, the House of Representatives has al-

1 See the XIIth Amendment to the Constitution.

2 Thirty Years' View, by a Senator of 30 years.   Vol. 1, pp. 46, 47.

most always been restricted in the exercise of these
functions to ascertaining the result of the ballot.

After the incidents that marked the elections of
Mr. Jefferson and of John Quincy Adams, it is
probable that, whenever this body is required to
choose between three candidates it will be satisfied
with the modest province of simply registering the
decision of the people.

Without here indicating other inconveniences
that the electoral colleges of the Union present, it
is proper to examine how far these constitutional
provisions have assisted a certain organization of
parties.

In the United States the entire sovereignty resides in the people. They delegate a portion of it
to the federal government, another portion to the
States. But it is proper to remark that they reserve the exclusive right to elect, mediately or immediately, the Federal and the State functionaries.
These all emanate from and are responsible to the
people. Thus, as is proved by facts, the representative is to such an extent governed by his constituents that he is almost always obliged to conform
to their wishes.

Moreover, the powerful organizations of political
parties come between the people and the representative. They nominate the candidates, so that the
sovereign has only to decide between the claims of
persons who, long prior to an election, are selected

by party conventions as worthy of the support of their adherents. At the beginning of the government, certain meetings of members of Congress (caucuses) nominated the presidential candidates. Thus, in 1800, the representatives of the Republican party of the House nominated Jefferson; in 1808 and in 1812, Madison; in 1816, Monroe, and in 1824, Crawford.

But in these meetings, formed exclusively of members of one party, the majority of votes only represented a small minority of the people. Separated from their constituents, and yet compelled to depend upon them, these representatives could not always expect to satisfy their wishes, and obtain their adhesion, so that this mode of nomination was never entirely accepted by the people. The legislatures of the most important States arrogated the right of designating the candidates, or at least insisted on participating in the exercise of it. Thus, in 1812, the Republican Legislature of New York chose a candidate in opposition to Mr. Madison, and in 1824 the name of General Jackson was presented by the Legislature of Tennessee. It need not then surprise us if, after the election of 1824, the different parties recognized their incapacity of making nominations through the instrumentality of their representatives in Congress.

There gradually arose, out of this state of things, the systems of conventions now in force, and since

1831 they have acted without interruption.[1] The Americans were, in this manner, led to create them.

A political party can scarcely exist in the United States without having adherents in almost all the States. It is, then, necessary to have a general organization which may apply to the whole nation, and a local organization in each State, county and township.

The Americans have succeeded in giving regular action to this complicated political machinery by exercising the right of peacefully assembling and forming associations for the maintenance of their political rights and opinions. The principle of free unions is guaranteed by the common law, and the use made of it by the Anglo-Saxons is so general that no one thinks of restricting it. When a party, then, is about to be formed, the persons who advocate the principles which are to be supported by it publish their programme; at the same time they invite all those who share their ideas to assemble in their respective districts and elect representatives to a convention, by which the contemplated party will be organized.

If the public respond, delegates will be chosen in each State, or at least in a certain number of States. They in their turn will unite and form a convention. This assembly then is constituted in

[1] Essays on Political Organization, published by the Union League of Philadelphia, pp. 64, 65.

conformity with customs that are almost invariable.
The credentials of the members are first verified
by a committee appointed *ad hoc.* The convention
declares, in a certain number of *resolutions*, its political principles, and sometimes also adopts an address
to the people. If the party considers itself strong
enough, or judges it to be opportune, candidates
are nominated, who are to be its standard-bearers,
and whose names are to be subsequently submitted
for popular suffrage. Finally, the convention constitutes a permanent organization or central committee, clothed with the power to convoke, when
it is deemed expedient, a new assembly, similar to
the one just held. In the interval, the committee
will control the party and watch over its interests.
The Republican party was organized in this manner
in 1836. Some determined abolitionists of New
York *nominated* a presidential candidate, and
although the anti-slavery movement was still confined to this State, they voted for him. At the
presidential election of 1840, the *"National Liberty Party"* was organized, and cast 7,000 votes.
At the election of 1844 it received 70,000. In
1848 its candidate, Mr. Van Buren, had nearly
250,000 votes. This organization increased at each
succeeding election until 1860, when its candidate,
Mr. Lincoln, was successful.

Let us now suppose a case where a party is so
far developed as to be on the point of becoming a

great national party. The period approaches for a presidential election; the committee of arrangements convokes a convention in which all the States are to be represented; it fixes the place of meeting, and determines, according to universally observed rules, the number of delegates that each State is to choose. The members of this party then publicly assemble in their respective wards or townships, and discuss the following questions :

1. What presidential candidate shall be nominated by the National Convention of the party? (In technical language the convention *nominates* a candidate, and the people *elect* him.)

2. What political programme shall be adopted?

After deciding these questions, this primary meeting (ward, township or county meeting), chooses a certain number of delegates, instructs them to sustain the ideas which have been adopted, and to uphold the candidate or candidates for whom it has expressed a preference.

Similar proceedings take place, almost at the same time, in the other counties which form the sub-divisions of the State. Then the citizens, chosen in this manner by all the primary assemblies, meet in their turn. They resume a second time the discussion of ideas which have been already debated; finally they appoint delegates to represent the State in the National Convention of the party. This is composed of delegations thus selected by a sort of

double election. Once united, this assembly har-
monizes, if we can make use of this expression,
all its discordant elements, chooses a candidate for
the presidency and makes known to the country its
political principles. Then, before finally adjourn-
ing, it forms a permanent committee, which will
retain its authority until the meeting of the next
convention. This committee consists of one or two
delegates taken from each State in the Union. At
the time of the appointment of delegates to the
National Convention, or at a subsequent meeting
of each State Convention, each party nominates
presidential electors, for whom the votes of the people are solicited, inasmuch as those who are elected
will be called upon to choose officially the President. [1]

In this way the persons who nominate a presidential candidate, and the electors who compose the
college, and cast the electoral vote of the State,
represent a common thought. They are both designated in a manner which subjects them to the
control of the same men. Party pressure is brought
to bear as well upon the members of the National
Convention as upon the presidential electors. Meanwhile the opposing party or parties have acted in
the same manner. After all the *nominations* have

[1] Sometimes it happens that the State Convention nominates only
the two presidential electors who represent the State at large in
the electoral college, and the others are chosen by the conventions
held in the congressional districts.

been made, and the programmes formally resolved upon, the electoral campaign, properly speaking, commences.

These very powerful combinations have been in turn the subject of enthusiastic praise and of severe criticism. In the first place, it cannot be denied that they have sufficed to constitute great political parties, given them peculiar vigor, and enforced the strictest discipline. On the other hand, it has been observed, and with much truth, that under this *régime* it is not really the association that governs, but the most insignificant minority that rules the majority.

"Party organizations, such as we have in this country, exist in no other, and are not necessary in a well-organized government.........The principal evils of our system of government grow out of these organizations, nominating conventions, and other party machinery devised to stimulate party spirit, to secure success at elections, either by fair or foul means, and to control the destinies of the country."

"Party organizations and machinery consist of national, state, county, city, ward and township committees, and committees for each congressional district for each political party, and township, ward and city meetings, county, state, district and national conventions for making nominations, discussing political questions, adopting resolutions, party

3

creeds and platforms, and appointing committees
for the succeeding year or term. The committees
call the meetings and conventions, provide for
holding them, procure and disseminate documents,
addresses, political tracts and other information
among the people; procure and distribute tickets
at the polls, and do various other things to obtain
votes and carry elections, some of which honest
men will do, and some of which they will not
do."

"The primary meetings of each party which
nominate township and ward officers, and appoint
delegates to city and county conventions, are generally composed of from ten to about fifty persons,
who are mostly politicians and aspirants to office,
or the friends of aspirants, and seldom comprise
more than from five to twenty per cent. of the
voters of the party for which they assume to act
.........all depending upon the action of the little
handful of party politicians attending the primary
meetings, and upon the delegates to county conventions appointed by them, the most of the voters
having no voice in selecting the candidates or
adopting the creed of either party."

"The primary meetings are attended by so few
persons, that it is generally easy for two or three
leaders to rally their friends and secure the appointment of such delegates as they wish; and conventions are easily packed to procure the nomination

of men who could not be nominated by the voice of the party fairly represented."

" .... This is often accomplished by the expenditure of considerable sums of money, and the profuse use of promises."............." Conventions come together simply to record the decisions of the leaders when they are united, and to determine by vote which faction or section is the strongest, when they are divided."

"Party leaders, deeply imbued with ambition and party spirit, desire an organization, frequent meetings and addresses, a party creed and a political faith, and also the establishment of some political dogmas, to distinguish them from other political parties, and to unite their friends and followers and stimulate their zeal. By such means they can determine what should be recognized as political orthodoxy, and are enabled to restrain freedom of opinion and individual liberty from endangering the unity of the party; and they can also maintain rigid party discipline, and confine the patronage of the party to the most zealous and active of the faithful; one of the main objects of the party leaders being to secure party zeal and fidelity, and activity and capacity to promote the success of the party, rather than the best interests of the country. ....A still further object is to form public opinion, and to educate and mould the public mind in accordance with the creed and dogmas of the party, in order to secure permanent success and party domination."[1]

The evils which have just been indicated are not the only ones. These assemblies are in general very numerously attended. Among those who compose them are found a great many inexperienced men, and a sufficient number of *politicians* to conduct the deliberations; they hold very few sessions. The delegates who attend are not in a situation to consult, to understand, or often even to know each other. It is not then to be wondered at that a handful of adroit managers do all the work, and that the convention generally does nothing more than give expression to their will. Such an assembly rarely accomplishes exactly what it wishes. Doubtless examples may be cited, tending to prove that the principle of association, thus applied, may be productive of good results; but, on the other hand, an intelligent and unprejudiced reader of the history of national conventions will not fail to perceive and appreciate all the faults and defects of the system.

For some time past the most sagacious observers have regarded these organizations as dangerous to the United States. In his great work, written

[1] The American System of Government, by Ezra Seaman, pp. 62 and succeeding.

several years before the breaking out of the civil war, Mr. Benton said : [1]

"I have seen the capacity of the people for self-government tried at many points, and always found it equal to the demands of the occasion. Two other trials, now going on, remain to be decided to settle the question of that capacity : 1st. The election of President, and whether that election is to be governed by the virtue and intelligence of the people, or to become the spoil of intrigue and corruption ? ....An irresponsible body," continues the author, "chiefly self-constituted, and mainly dominated by professional office-seekers and office-holders, have usurped the election of President (for the nomination is the election, so far as the party is concerned), and always making it with a view to their own profit in the monopoly of office and plunder."

The second danger pointed out by Mr. Benton, and which it is not necessary to investigate here, was the question of slavery.[2]

It results from the experience of the past forty years in particular, that the organization of parties identifies the President with that one which has elected him. He becomes, by the very fact of his

---

[1] Mr. Thomas H. Benton was for thirty years a United States Senator. He has related in two large volumes the events which he witnessed. This great work, entitled "Thirty Years' View," is very useful to consult, although Mr. Benton has too often recorded in his writings the passionate impressions which he received in the struggles of the day.

[2] See Thirty Years' View, Vol. II., p. 787.

nomination by a convention, the official representative, if not the chief, of this party. By it he obtains power. By it he will be supported and will govern. It is scarcely possible for him to disconnect himself from it, and up to the present time every President attempting it has failed. Almost always designated by *politicians,* and presented by them for the popular vote, he is, even before the election, united to them by the strongest ties, and when he enters on the discharge of his functions, woe betide him if he forget those to whom he owes nearly all his success.

If there be a man who, of late years, has been called by public sentiment to the chief magistracy of the United States, that man is assuredly General Grant. The Republican party, without doubt, adopted him in 1868, but this choice was in reality enjoined upon it by public opinion; so that for once the candidate gained the presidential mansion free from entangling engagements. He seemed at first resolved to take advantage of this propitious circumstance, and to maintain, at least as far as was practicable, his independence. His first acts clearly denoted this intention, but unhappily he soon reached the conclusion that he must renounce the attempt. He became impressed with the conviction that he could not dispense with the support of the politicians, and he was obliged to come to an understanding with them.

If the close relations which exist between the President and the chiefs of his party often give much vigor to his administration; if in this way he avoids many conflicts with Congress, and secures the undivided support of a powerful organization, spread throughout the entire country, he on the other hand incurs heavy obligations, and must reward services which have been rendered him. Hence his dependence; hence also his weakness. How many compromises is he not required to make, how many interests is he not compelled to satisfy !

The President is then placed in a situation wherein the political organization which put him in power actively supports him, provided, that it receives in exchange all the gratifications and rewards to which it considers itself entitled. In order to govern the country, he must make habitual concessions to his party, which acts, so to say, as his executive agents; if he withdraws from it, his power will immediately diminish, and he will, ere long, become the victim of those with whom he fails to act in concert.

The administrative disorder which reigns in the United States aggravates this condition of things; almost all public offices are considered as belonging to the victorious party; "to the victors," says the American maxim, "belong the spoils." Therefore, at the beginning of an administration, those who have contributed to assure the success of the electoral campaign, consider themselves entitled to demand a division of the offices as an undoubted right. The President has to meet innumerable demands, and as he cannot overlook active party services, the most annoying difficulties are thereby entailed upon him, and they will increase with the growing population and resources of the country. The creation of public offices, rendered necessary by the late civil war, greatly enlarged the patronage of the government, and added, in a corresponding degree, to the embarrassments of him who dispenses it.

For some time past statesmen and publicists have sought the means of putting an end to this state of things. They have thought that if they succeeded in rendering national conventions useless, they could break up the machinery of that political organization which incites and regulates party movements, even in the counties and townships. With this view, the suppression of the electoral colleges has been proposed.

They could, without difficulty, prove that this institution, to which, in theory, appertains the right of choosing the President, has in practice no real power whatever; that, acting always in obedience to special and imperative instructions, it is consequently useless. In 1824 a Senator said that the objections against a direct election by the people,

which prevailed with the members of the convention of 1787, had already nearly lost their importance.   An attempt was made at the session of
1825–26 to procure an amendment to the Constitution.   A committee composed of nine members
was appointed by the Senate, which agreed upon
a proposition of amendment.   The prominent features of this plan of election are, 1. The abolition
of electors and the direct vote of the people; 2. A
second election between the two highest on each
list, when no one has a majority of the whole; 3.
Uniformity in the mode of election.

The advantages of this plan would be to get rid
of all the machinery by which the *selection* of their
two first magistrates is now taken out of the hands
of the people.   If any one received a majority
of the whole number of districts in the first election, then the democratic principle, the majority to
govern, is satisfied.   If no one receives such a majority, then the first election stands for a popular
nomination of the two highest—a nomination by
the people themselves.   But to provide for a possible contigency—too improbable ever to occur
—and to save, in that case, the trouble of a third
popular election, a resort to the House of Representatives is allowed, it being *nationally* unimportant which is elected where the candidates were
exactly equal in the public estimation.   The plan
was unanimously recommended by the committee.

But it did not receive the requisite support of
two-thirds of the Senate to carry it through that
body.[1]

The 8th of December, 1829, General Jackson
recommended to Congress the adoption of a similar
measure: "To the people," said the message, "belongs the right of electing their chief magistrate;
it was never designed that their choice should, in
any case, be defeated, either by the intervention of
electoral colleges, or by the agency confided, under
certain contingencies, to the House of Representatives........." [2]

In 1844 the question again came up, but it does
not appear at that time to have occupied the attention of Congress as it had done twenty years before.
Since then it has often been agitated, without ever
having been made the subject of earnest investigation. In the course of the session of 1871-72,
Mr. Sumner reproduced it, in the following terms:

"WHEREAS, According to the existing system,
the President of the United States, instead of being
chosen directly by the people, is chosen by the intervention of electoral colleges in the several States;
and

"WHEREAS, This system, *besides excluding the
people from a direct vote in the choice of President,*

1 Thirty Years' View, pp. 78-79.

2 See "The Addresses and Messages of the Presidents of the
United States." New York, 1842. P. 359.

*is operated by the caucus or convention, an irrespon-
sible body, unknown to the law or Constitution, where
a few persons by combination, and sometimes by intrigue or corruption, succeed in putting forward a
candidate who becomes forthwith the exclusive representative of a political party, so that the triumph of
the party assures his election; and*

".WHEREAS, *The caucus or convention, after being
the engine for the nomination of President, allowing
the people a little more than to record its will, becomes
the personal instrument of the President when elected,
giving him a dictatorial power, which he may employ
in reducing the people to conformity with his purposes
and promoting his re-election,* all of which is hostile
to good government, and of evil example ; and

"WHEREAS, The existing system of choosing a
President, *besides being highly artificial and cumber-
some, is radically defective and unrepublican,* inasmuch as it fails to secure for each voter the opportunity of declaring for the candidate of his choice,
and in its operation substitutes therefor the dictation of a caucus or convention."

Such are the reasons assigned by Mr. Sumner
in the preamble to the resolutions which he offered
looking to the abolition of the system now in force.
They recapitulate very clearly the objections to
which it has given rise.

It is impossible to say whether the United
States will soon adopt any project of electoral re-

form. It is, however, probable that the existing system has not yet outlived its time. Its inherent faults must first be more generally known.

Such are the varied experiences of the United States regarding the presidential election. The convention of 1787 was right in withholding from the House of Representatives the right to elect the President. Had it done otherwise, one of two things would have happened—either the House would have received imperative instructions from its constituents—it would itself have been elected, in view of the presidential choice to be made by it, or it would have become a central point of intrigues. Party spirit would have distracted it, and each candidate would have employed every means at his disposal to secure votes. Never would an election have been less free and unbiased.

The system adopted by the Philadelphia Convention, which, with the amendment of 1803, has been maintained to the present day, has encouraged the organization of parties. At the same time, as has been seen, the electoral colleges have lost even the right of expressing a personal preference. They have been reduced to simply registering the popular verdict. In this, then, the election, through a second agency, has completely failed.

The direct election of the chief magistrate by the people remains to be tried. It is impossible to foresee the practical result of this experiment.

The choice of a President determines for four years the general policy of the United States. The convention that designates the candidate whose nomination is subsequently ratified by the people, has marked out a programme. This programme has been explained by all the " stump-speakers" of the party, and adopted by the innumerable local conventions held about the same time. The party has in this way expressed its ideas upon the situation ; the candidate for the presidency has formally given in his adhesion, and his honor, as a public man, is pledged to its execution.

Once elected, the President knows then the policy he is to pursue. If no exceptional or disturbing causes occur to distract the public mind, it is easy to tell from the day that he enters upon his duties what will be his line of conduct. But at a critical juncture matters do not take place in the same manner ; if new political questions arise, a programme previously decided on cannot have foreseen them. Then it becomes his duty to discern the direction of that public opinion, which alone has supreme authority to sit in judgment on his action. Within these limits he has full scope to display all the qualities of a statesman. As he is not politically amenable to any jurisdiction, he may act with entire freedom, provided he does not violate the laws with a criminal intent. Even if he deem it best either to offer a momentary resistance to public opinion, or to anticipate it, he is at liberty to do so. However, he should never lose sight of the party chiefs, who have borne him into power; he must at all hazards avoid an estrangement from them.

Notwithstanding these conditions of political dependence on a party, and an ultimate responsibility to the people, public opinion allows the greatest liberty of action to the President. He is in a position to act with vigor, and up to a certain point his movements may be independent. It cannot be doubted that this authority is indispensable to the development of the United States, as well as to the maintenance of liberty.

The election of the Vice-president of the republic requires some special remarks. By the terms of the Constitution he performs, for the greater part of the time, unimportant functions. He presides over the deliberations of the Senate, but cannot take part in them, nor has he a vote, except in rare instances, in which the members are equally divided. However, under certain circumstances he may be called to the presidency. "In case of the removal of the President from office, or of his death, resignation, or inability to discharge the powers and duties of the said office, the same shall devolve on the Vice-president." This clause of the fundamental law[1] has already taken effect three

---

[1] Constitution, Article II., Section 1, ¶ 5.

times in the history of the United States. At the death of General Harrison, Mr. Tyler succeeded him; Mr. Fillmore became President at the death of General Taylor, and finally, when Mr. Lincoln was assassinated, Mr. Johnson took his place.

Perplexing questions relative to the then Constitutional status of the Vice-president have arisen. Some assert that he administers the Executive Power, being simply charged with its functions; others, on the contrary, maintain that, by the very fact of a change of persons, he becomes in deed and of right President of the United States. This difference of opinion is not unimportant; however, as the question is yet in abeyance, there is no reason for dwelling upon it now. On the contrary, it is useful to consider all the bearings of the arrangement which may eventually place him in the executive chair.

On the three occasions in which the Vice-president succeeded the President, disagreements more or less serious existed between the executive and the legislative power.

The administration of Mr. Tyler was very troubled, and although Mr. Fillmore did not encounter so violent an opposition, yet he met with very serious embarrassments; while under Mr. Johnson matters proceeded to the utmost extremity. The experience of the United States on this subject is, then, very far from giving satisfactory results.

It is not, moreover, difficult to see why this arrangement did not succeed. In the first place, the Vice-president and President are nominated by the same convention. The important man has been chosen for the first office ; but almost always there will be found, in assemblies thus constituted, a minority who are not wholly pleased with the nomination. These discontented persons must be satisfied—and the second place ·is given to the candidate selected by them.

It frequently occurs that the Vice-president does not exactly represent the ideas or interests which dictated the first choice. Doubtless, the system in use offers advantages in regard to the election. As the two candidates have many points of difference, they supplement and at times strengthen each other. But that which may be useful during the canvass may eventually become a cause of very serious embarrassment. In case the Vice-president is suddenly called upon to exercise the office of chief magistrate, it is easy to foresee the consequences growing out of this change of persons. Although he has been elected by a majority of the people, yet he does not the less for all that represent, in many respects, the views of a certain minority. If he remain faithful to them, he may find himself in open opposition to his own party. Besides, from the moment when the people elect a President this candidate alone is before the public eye, and it is to him that the authority is delegated by the vote of the country. So, in this case, the question is not simply to ascertain the degree of opposition that one man is able to make to the collective power of Congress.

"If the President is strong, it is because the people who, by their suffrage, have raised him to his place, are behind him, holding up his hands, speaking with his voice, sustaining him in his high duties, that the President has the place and can maintain it under the Constitution.............So this great power does not present any danger to the country, and the President may exercise it safely, because he is supported by the people who have just given him so striking a proof of their confidence in calling him to the chief magistracy."[1] If, on the contrary, he who fills the executive functions has not been chosen by a popular election made with the view of confiding this power to him directly .... "then at once discord, dislocation, deficiency, difficulty show themselves; then at once the great powers of the office, which were consonant with a free constitution and with the supremacy of popular will, by the fact that for a brief term the breath of life of the continuing favor of the people gave them efficiency and strength, find no support in fact. Then it is, that in the criti-

---

[1] Impeachment Trial of Andrew Johnson, pp. 721, 722; argument of Hon. William M. Evarts.

4

cisms of the press, in the estimate of public men, in the views of the people, these great powers, strictly in trust and within the Constitution, seem to be despotic and personal."[1]

Finally, all the aspirants, all those who are interested in the public service, or who established relations with the late President, find themselves in an awkward position as regards his successor. If then a Vice-president, who is suddenly called upon to occupy so different a situation, fails to show the requisite wisdom and prudence, if he does not possess the personal qualities necessary to maintain peace, contests must inevitably ensue, and then the executive falls into an exceptional state of weakness.

Thus the constitutional provision, in virtue of which the Vice-president may eventually take the place of the President, has caused the United States, up to the present time, inconveniences of the gravest nature; and, although this question has not as yet attracted public attention to the extent that it deserves, it is possible that sooner or later it may become the subject of thorough discussion. However that may be, this provision ought not to be imitated elsewhere. If a nation should adopt "the republican form of government," it would be more to its advantage to declare that if the Presi-

___

[1] Impeachment Trial of Andrew Johnson, pp. 721, 722; argument of Hon. William M. Evarts.

dent elect ceases, from any reason whatever, to exercise his functions, the presiding officer of one of the legislative chambers should temporarily serve, and be required to order the election of a successor with the least possible delay.

CHAPTER II.

CONSTITUTION OF THE EXECUTIVE POWER.

WE must not for a moment lose sight of the fact that the people have not delegated all their powers to the Federal Government. The latter is only sovereign within a restricted sphere of action prescribed by the Constitution. It is, then, impossible to compare it with the governments of other States. In England, Prussia, Russa and France, the central power, whatever it may be, represents the whole national sovereignty, while in the United States the Federal Government only represents a part of it, and is confined to the exercise of the powers enumerated by the fundamental law.

There is no necessity for presenting here the considerations which induced the Philadelphia Convention to adopt this system; but it is important to remark that it would be almost impossible for other nations to make a similar division of powers. Indeed, a country must be placed in peculiar circumstances to prevent an absorption of all authority by the general government.

We will now look into the Constitution of the

United States, and see in what manner it divides between several departments the sovereign prerogatives conferred upon the Federal Government. It creates an executive, a legislative and a judicial department, and provides that they shall be all three " co-ordinate and independent" ; or, to use the words of a decision of the Supreme Court, the several branches of the government " are co-ordinate in degree to the extent of the powers delegated to each of them. Each, in the exercise of its powers, is independent of the other, but all, rightfully done by either, is binding upon the others." [1]

It was thus the purpose of the convention to unite the three powers in such manner that each of them might exert a constitutional control within its own orbit, and at the same time that neither should have a marked ascendency over the others. It neglected nothing in order to avoid an absorption, or even a gradual concentration, of all powers in one, and labored to assure the independence of each. To this end it declared, in effect, that the President, or a civil officer, should not be impeached except for high crimes and misdemeanors, and that no executive agents should be held politically responsible to Congress. On the other hand, the President could never dissolve the Congress, or even suspend the course of its deliberations.

At the same time the convention calculated that

1 18 Howard. Dodge *vs.* Woolsey, p. 347.

personal motives would play an important part, and that the men who would form one of the three powers would be naturally called upon to defend its privileges and maintain its prerogatives. Thus, after having explained how human ambition would contribute to preserve each branch of the government in its constitutional rights, the "Federalist" observed that, in order to avoid a predominance of legislative authority, it was necessary to divide the Legislature into two branches, as distinct as possible. But this did not appear to be sufficient; the Executive Power must still be strengthened, and, nevertheless, all these precautions would not have reassured the authors of the "Federalist," if they had not found a new guaranty in the very division of the sovereignty between the Federal government and the State governments. It was well, in their opinion, that power should be divided at first between two distinct governments, and then be distributed among the several departments of each. Hence this partial delegation of sovereignty. Hence these three powers, at once co-ordinate and independent, which derive their authority from the Constitution, and which, while they act in concert, yet serve to counterpoise each other.

This leads us to explain how the Executive Power was organized, in order to assure its co-operation with the two other departments, and at the same time to guaranty its independence. The

first care of the convention was to give to the
President as much strength as possible. [1]

" There is an idea," says the "Federalist," "which
is not without its advocates, that a vigorous executive is inconsistent with the genius of republican
government. The enlightened well-wishers to this
species of government must at least hope that the
supposition is destitute of foundation, since they
can never .admit its truth without, at the same
time, admitting the condemnation of their own
principles. Energy in the executive is a leading
character in the definition of good government. It
is essential to the protection of the community
against foreign attacks; it is not less essential to
the steady administration of the laws, to the protection of property against those irregular and
high-handed combinations which sometimes inter-
rupt the ordinary course of justice, to the security
of liberty against the enterprises and assaults of
ambition, of faction, and anarchy"........." A feeble
executive implies a feeble execution of the government. A feeble execution is but another phrase for
a bad execution, and a government badly executed,
whatever it may be in theory, must be, in practice,
a bad government."

It remains to be seen what are the essential elements of that energy which is necessary to the
Executive Power. According to the "Federalist"

1 See the " Federalist," pp. 333–364.

they are, first, unity; secondly, duration; thirdly, an adequate provision for its support, and fourthly, competent powers.

"Those politicians and statesmen," adds the "Federalist," "who have been the most celebrated for the soundness of their principles, and for the justness of their views, have declared in favor of a single Executive and a numerous Legislature. They have, with great propriety, considered energy as the most necessary qualification of the former, and have regarded this as most applicable to power in a single hand, while they have, with equal propriety, considered the latter as best adapted to deliberation and wisdom, and best calculated to conciliate the confidence of the people, and to secure their privileges and interests........."

"That unity is conducive to energy will not be disputed. Decision, activity, secrecy and dispatch will generally characterize the proceedings of one man in a much more eminent degree than the proceedings of any greater number, and in proportion as the number is increased, these qualities will be diminished."

If the Executive Power was confided to two or three persons the people would be deprived of the strongest guarantees which can be found in the delegation of power. Thanks to unity, public opinion is able to scrutinize the President, and to determine upon whom to direct its censure; the people are also capable of determining the responsibility which may attach to their mandatary, and, if need be, they know whom to punish. "But in a republic, where every magistrate ·ought to be personally responsible for his behavior in office.........the propriety of a council not only ceases to apply but turns against the institution."[1]

"Duration in office has been mentioned as the second requisite to the energy of the executive authority. This has relation to two objects : to the personal firmness of the executive magistrate in the employment of his constitutional powers, and to the stability of the system of administration which may have been adopted under his auspices. With regard to the first, it must be evident that the longer the duration in office, the greater will be the probability of obtaining so important an advantage. It is a general principle of human nature that a man will be interested in whatever he possesses, in proportion to the firmness or precariousness of the tenure by which he holds it; will be less attached to what he holds by a momentary or uncertain title......... This remark is not less applicable to a political privilege, or honor, or trust, than to any ordinary article of property. The inference from it is, that a man acting in the capacity of chief magistrate, under a consciousness that in a very short time he *must* lay down his office, will be

1 The "Federalist," p. 486 *et. seq.*

apt to feel himself too little interested in it to hazard any material censure or perplexity from the
independent exertion of his powers, or from encoun-
tering the ill humors, however transient, which
may happen to prevail, either in a considerable part
of the society itself, or even in a predominant faction of the legislative body. If the case should
only be that he *might* lay it down, unless continued
by a new choice, and if he should be desirous of
being continued, his wishes, conspiring with his
fears, would tend still more powerfully to corrupt
his integrity or debase his fortitude. In either
case, feebleness and irresolution must be the characteristics of the station."

"There are some who would be inclined to regard the servile pliancy of the executive to a prevailing current, either in the community or in the
Legislature, as its best recommendation. But such
men entertain very crude notions, as well as of the
purposes for which government was instituted, as
of the true means by which the public happiness
may be promoted. The republican principle demands that the deliberate sense of the community
should govern the conduct of those to whom they
intrust the management of their affairs; but it does
not require an unqualified complaisance to every
sudden breeze of passion, or to every transient im-
pulse which the people may receive from the arts
of men who flatter their prejudices to betray their

interests. It is a just observation that the people commonly *intend the public good.* This often applies to their very errors. But their good sense would despise the adulator who should pretend that they always *reason right* about the *means* of promoting it. They know from experience ,that they some-times err, and the wonder is, that they so seldom err as they do, beset, as they continually are, by the wiles of parasites and sycophants ; by the snares of the ambitious, the avaricious, the desperate ; by the artifices of men who possess their confidence more than they deserve it; and of those who seek to possess rather than to deserve it. When occa-sions present themselves, in which the interests of the people are at variance with their inclinations, it is the duty of the persons whom they have ap-pointed to be the guardians of those interests, to withstand the temporary delusion in order to give them time and opportunity for more cool and sedate reflection. Instances might be cited in which a conduct of this kind has saved the people from very fatal consequences of their own mistakes, and has procured lasting monuments of their gratitude to the men who had courage and magnanimity enough to serve them at the peril of their displea-sure........."[1]

Nor should the executive yield to the caprices of the Legislature. "It may sometimes stand in op-

[1] The "Federalist," p. 496 *et seq.*

position to the former; and at other times the people may be entirely neutral. In either supposition, it is certainly desirable that the executive should be in a situation to dare to act his own opinion with vigor and decision."

If it is necessary to divide power between different branches of the government, it is equally indispensable to guarantee the independence of each What good purpose would be subserved by separating the executive and the judicial from the legislative power, if the first two were so constituted, as to be constrained to obey implicitly the third? In such a case a division would be purely nominal, and none of the expected results would be realized. "It is one thing to be subordinate to the laws, and another to be dependent on the legislative body. The first comports with, the last violates, the fundamental principles of good government; and whatever may be the forms of the Constitution, unites all powers in the same hands.........In governments purely republican this tendency is almost irresistible. The representatives of the people, in a popular assembly, seem sometimes to fancy that they are the people themselves, and betray strong symptoms of impatience and disgust at the least sign of opposition from any other quarter, as if the exercise of its rights by either the executive or judiciary were a breach of their privilege and an outrage to their dignity. They often appear disposed to exert an imperious control over the other departments."[1]

As regards the duration of the presidential term, the Federalist asks if four years suffices to give to the Executive Power that vigor which is essential to it? and in reply. expresses its apprehensions: "Between the commencement and termination of such a period there would always be," said Hamil ton, " a considerable interval, in which the prospect of annihilation would be sufficiently remote not to have an improper effect upon the conduct of a man endued with a tolerable portion of fortitude, and in which he might reasonably promise himself that there would be time enough before it arrived to make the community sensible of the propriety of the measures he might be inclined to pursue. Though it is probable that, as he approached the moment when the public were, by a new election, to signify their sense of his conduct, his confidence, and with it his firmness, would decline."

And in the third place, the executive authority must be maintained, and with this view the President is to receive a salary in proportion to the importance of his functions. Had this point been overlooked in the Constitution, thought the authors of the "Federalist," the separation of the executive and legislative branches of the government would be quite illusory. If Congress had a

1 The "Federalist," p. 499.

discretionary power over the compensation of the chief magistrate, he would cease to be independent. The legislative power could in a measure starve him out. Therefore the Constitution prescribes that " The President of the United States shall, at stated times, receive for his service a compensation, *which shall neither be increased, nor diminished, during the period for which he shall have been elected;* and he *shall not receive within that period any other emolument* from the United States, or any of them.".

Thus, at the time of his election, Congress determines once for all what pecuniary provision shall be made for him during his term of office.

Finally, in order to give him that vigor which is indispensable to the efficient exercise of his functions, he must have the requisite prerogatives. The Constitution defines them; but this is not the place to examine them in detail.

Thus the framers of the Constitution determined to assure to the Executive Power both independence and vigor; to organize it, in a.word, in such manner that it should possess all the requisite qualities for the conduct of affairs.[1] Results attest that their plan was well conceived.

Notwithstanding the numerous struggles that have taken place between the three powers, these co-ordinate and independent branches of the Federal government have been able to co-exist.

1 The " Federalist," p. 86 *et seg.*

Experience also proves that (thanks to the term of office fixed by the Constitution for the President and for Congress) a contest between them would never be pushed to extreme consequences, and that the people, as sovereign judge of the questions at issue between the contending parties, would almost always be able to intervene in time.

However, the Constitutional Convention was not able to organize a system of political responsibility. Doubtless, it provided that all federal functionaries, the President not excepted, might be impeached by the House of Representatives and tried by the Senate; but, as will be seen in the course of this work, this procedure applies solely to the func·tionary who has committed a crime or a misdemeanor which a law of the United States defines and punishes. His criminal responsibility is confined within those limits.

It is true that the President is morally responsible to the people; public opinion may always condemn him. But if the entire nation, as if with one voice, should arraign and censure him, his legal situation would in no wise be modified. In fact, he would probably have lost all his moral authority, but in law, he would none the less continue to exercise to the fullest extent all the inherent powers of the presidential office.

It is said that it would have been otherwise, had the Constitution established ministerial responsibility. A council, according to the doctrine of a well-known school, would have sufficed to harmonize these independent powers; nevertheless the United States were right in rejecting the system.

The President is elected by the people; the Constitution confers upon him large powers. What purpose would this election subserve, and of what avail would be these powers, if the chief magistrate was obliged to surround himself with a council, organized for the purpose of governing in his name? He would then necessarily become the instrument of Congress, and be constrained to yield incessantly to its wishes. His situation would soon be rendered intolerable; elected by, and morally responsible to, the people, he would be compelled to let his council govern in order to satisfy the legislative power! Had this been the case the executive authority would have almost entirely disappeared. The supreme power would then abide in Congress; and this is precisely what a democratic people should above all things avoid. If the appropriate province of legislative assemblies is yet but imperfectly understood, the cause of the errors which prevail in this regard may be readily found. For nearly a century the constitutional and parliamentary school of Europe has to some extent based its doctrines on English tradition. Doubtless, in the great British monarchy, Parliament has been able to occupy the first place; but the Executive Power is there hereditary and irresponsible, and therefore bears, in this respect, no resemblance to the elective presidency. Again, English parliamentary authority has for a long time been engrossed by a small number of persons. The heads of aristocratic fam-. ilies have almost to the present day governed the affairs of the nation. How different the conditions imposed by a democratic society upon the legislative assemblies. The latter may doubtless be well qualified to pass laws and discuss the budget of receipts and expenditures ; at least up to the present time no substitute for them has been found in a free government, but history furnishes scarcely an instance of their capacity to govern the country which they represent.

In the United States, if the administration of public affairs devolved on Congress, it is very questionable whether a judicious, use would long be made of its authority. Disorder in transacting them would probably soon be manifest. Now, it must not be forgotten that disorder—and this is specially the case in democratic nations—is essentially incompatible with liberty. Forced to choose between anarchy and despotism, they will always select the latter alternative. In this respect, they are infinitely more impressionable than aristocracies, and the framers of the Constitution were fully aware of the fact. Their resolution to exclude the plan of an executive council was, however, only

5

reached after long debates. The English parliamentary system had great prestige in their eyes, and their refusal to adopt it must be ascribed to their conviction, that it was incompatible with the existence of a republican government. Being thus constrained to give to the executive branch the unity, vigor and powers which are indispensable to it, and, at the same time, shield it from political responsibility to Congress, they preferred to submit to the great inconveniences which might result from the sacrifice. At the same time they limited the presidential term to four years. The people, by the exercise of their sovereign power, can correct, at the end of this period, the error which they may have committed at its commencement.

If we reflect, however, on the conditions under which the President is nominated by a convention and elected by the people, we cannot avoid the conclusion, that if the hereditary transmission of power is exposed to great hazards, those incident to a popular election are perhaps equally great. And yet the people ought to be willing to acquiesce in a choice imprudently made. The Executive Power is confided to their selected agent for four years. If they have been deceived by him, they must quietly submit until the expiration of his term. It is only on these conditions that the republic can be maintained.

Another question, almost as complicated as the

preceding ones, the re-eligibility of the President, was also presented for the consideration of the framers of thé Constitution. They determined it in the affirmative. Hamilton thus explains in the "Federalist" the motives which led them to this result :

"One ill effect of the exclusion would be a diminution of the inducements to good behavior. There are few men who would not feel much less zeal in the discharge of a duty, when they were conscious that the advantages of the station with which it was connected must be relinquished at a determinate period, than when they were permitted to entertain a hope of *obtaining* by *meriting* a continuance of them. This position will not be contested so long as it is admitted that the desire of reward is one of the strongest incentives of human conduct, or that the best security for the fidelity of mankind is to make their interest coincide with their duty."[1]

At the same time Hàmilton was of opinion that in this way the President would not allow himself to be influenced by unworthy designs, which might even lead to ideas of usurpation.

"A third ill effect of the exclusion would be the depriving the community of the advantage of the experience gained by the chief magistrate in the exercise of his office..........What more desirable or

[1] Tho "Federallst," p. 502 *et seq.*

more essential than this quality in the governors
of nations? Can it be wise to put this desirable
and essential quality under the ban of the Constitution, and to declare that the moment it is acquired
its possessor shall be compelled to abandon the
station in which it was acquired, and to which it
was adapted?.........And yet, what would result
from such exclusion?—the banishing men from sta-
tions in which, in certain emergencies of the State,
their presence might be of the greatest moment to
the public interest and safety. There is no nation
which has not, at one period or another, experienced an absolute necessity of the services of particular men in particular situations; perhaps it
would not be too strong to say, to the preservation
of its political existence." [1]

To those who assumed that the very fact of
exclusion would assure a greater degree of independence to the chief magistrate and a better security
to the people, Hamilton replied by presenting considerations of a nature to show, in his view, the
futility of such objections. As is known, the constitutional provision has been maintained to the
present day ; the President has always been re-
eligible. However, guided by the example of
Washington, who had himself refused the third
election, the practice has been to re-elect the President but once.

[1] The "Federalist," p. 505 *et seq.*

Nevertheless, in 1829, General Jackson recommended to Congress the adoption of a constitutional amendment, declaring that the President could not be elected a second time.[1] Since then the question has been often agitated, and the disadvantages resulting from the system now in force have been pointed out from time to time by leading statesmen.

It has been said that in every country the inquiry naturally suggests itself, whether the ruler of the nation, holding in his hands the resources of the Executive Power, is an ordinary candidate? When the patronage and authority vested in him by the Constitution be considered, it is obvious that, in an electoral contest, he occupies a different position from that of a private citizen, soliciting the people to confer upon him the first office in their gift.

The party which aids in securing the re-election of the President is also placed in an exceptional situation. It is supported by the office-holders, who place at its disposal all the influence of the government. If we suppose an administration as regular and as well organized as could be desired, yet even then the means of action that the President may use will be immense.

As has been elsewhere very justly remarked, if

---

[1] See his first annual message, in the compilation entitled, "Address and Messages, of the President," New York, 1842.

magistracies, traditionally constituted and irremovable, can assure but imperfectly the independence of the incumbents, what will be the result when functionaries are interested, whose official existence, or at least advancement, may depend on the executive chief.

The advocates of the re-eligibility of the President affirm, in reply to these criticisms, that the public service might and should be organized and regulated so as to protect dependent functionaries from any pressure that he might bring to bear upon them. Nothing is less sound than this argument, for he will always have means of influence powerful enough to constrain them to conform to his wishes: When he desires a re-election, he employs in the attainment of that object all the means that the Constitution gives him. If he has conceived this design for some time previous to the commencement of the presidential campaign, he calls around him those partisans who favor his wishes, and distributes amongst them his political patronage, so as to acquire in the party, which has already elected him, that aid which is indispensable to his purpose. By the employment of all the resources at the disposal of the administration, as many journals as possible are enlisted for the candidate for re-election. Gradually the office-holders organize all over the country primary meetings, which are skillfully composed of devoted partisans. A united effort is then made, and a national convention, consisting of delegates carefully chosen, ratifies the decision made a long time before by the chief of the Executive Power.

From the moment of the nomination the strength of the party combines with the administrative organization of the United States. They are blended to such a degree, that their separate existence ceases for a time ; then the partisans can no longer be distinguished from the functionaries, for they are all transformed into electioneering agents. Without having witnessed such a spectacle, it is doubtful if a European can appreciate its character ; he would find it difficult to understand the extent to which matters are pushed. When the electoral struggle begins, neutrality is no longer permitted. If a politician tries to preserve his independence and at the same time remain in full fellowship with his party, he is soon forced by its discipline to express his sentiments, and if he openly revolts against this tyranny, he will be denounced as a traitor, no matter what signal services he may have previously rendered. His conscientious resistance to the exactions and intrigues of party leaders will soon shroud in oblivion all his past efforts and sacrifices.

Such proceedings have an inevitable tendency to corrupt the public morals. Their recurrence, then, must be prevented. This can only be effectually accomplished by a constitutional amendment prohibiting the re-election of the President. Much reliance cannot be safely placed upon his patriotic abnegation. During his first term he has before him the history of his predecessors, and beholds them, so to say, divided into two classes, in one of which are found those who held the office for eight years, and at their head is the name of Washington. In the other, are those whose administration was not always crowned with success, and it is natural that he should seek to be ranked with the first. The more elevated his sentiments, the more will he cherish a legitimate ambition, coupled with an earnest desire to prolong the duration of his service and to perpetuate his name. In this case, the noblest impulses of human nature will prompt him to solicit the honor of a new lease of official life.

Doubtless such exceptional circumstances may occur as to render the re-election of the President up to a certain point a public necessity. But too much importance must not be attached to what may be said in this respect. If ever an election occurred during a crisis, it was that of 1864, which returned Mr. Lincoln to a second term. The electoral campaign took place during the war, and as he himself said in words which were at least quaintly original, "it is not prudent to swap horses in the middle of a river." However, it is very doubtful if his rare gifts and the prestige of his

honored name were indispensable to the safety
of the Union. In 1864, even under circumstances of such gravity, the Republican party could
without danger have elected another President.
He would have followed the same line of conduct.
Doubtless, the re-election of Mr. Lincoln gave an
emphatic popular sanction to the policy of abolish-
ing slavery and waging war until all armed opposition should cease; but any other candidate, chosen
with a view to this programme, would have probably executed it. The support of the Republican
party would have been given to the elect of the
nation, and the effect of a change of persons would
not have compromised the triumph of the arms of
the Union. As the Constitution permitted the
re-election of Mr. Lincoln, his success offered great
advantages; but if that instrument had interdicted
it, the United States would have conformed without
serious embarrassment to the law of exclusion.

On the other hand, it cannot be denied that a
term of four years, without a possibility of re-election, is not long enough. In fact, the President
elect enters almost always upon his duties without
much experience in public affairs. He requires at
least six months of initiation to render them famil-
iar to him. He is scarcely then in the exercise of
full authority, and, unfortunately, only preserves it
during two years and a half. When the fourth
year of his term commences, the country enters

upon a new presidential crisis. This affects the
political situation to such a degree that, up to the
close of the electoral campaign, something like a
suspension in the life of the government takes
place. After the election of his successor, the
President still remains in office four months, but
he then confines himself almost exclusively to closing up current business.

Thus, many thoughtful persons have been struck
by the inconveniences arising out of the short duration of the term. They have, therefore, proposed
to prolong it by two years, and at the same time
render the President ineligible. There is no reason
to doubt the happy results of this reform. He
would have four years and a half of full authority;
and this arrangement would agree very well with
the exigencies of a democratic society. · In a country where a disposition to watch the progress of
public affairs and the conduct of public men per-
vades all classes, where criticism is so keen and so
personal, it is difficult for one in an elevated official
position to resist for a longer time the incessant
attacks of which he is the object. Do as he may,
he is soon worn out.

But, then, if the President remained in office six,
or even eight years, the essential conditions to the
existence of his authority could not be modified,
for in that event he would not be surrounded by a
parliamentary cabinet responsible to Congress. It

is proper also to observe, by the way, that when
Hamilton proposed to elect a President for life, and
thus sought to approach toward an hereditary royalty, he was not in favor of surrounding that officer with a council taken from the deliberative assemblies; he maintained that this power should be
active, energetic, and clothed with large authority.

However that may be, it is evident that if an
amendment to the Constitution should extend the
presidential term to six years, it would not remedy
grave embarrassments. Even with this prolonged
duration a lamentable instability in the chief magistracy would still exist. But is not this very instability inherent in democratic institutions, and
should not a nation ardently devoted to them cheerfully accept their disadvantages when they reap
their benefits? Moreover, in a society so constituted politics must necessarily be confined to domestic
exigencies, which occur from day to day. All
questions of foreign policy must be studiously
avoided. Certain aristocracies have been able to
prepare slowly the greatness of the country they
governed; generations have succeeded each other
and transmitted an immutable tradition; monarchies have done the same thing with equal success; the father has taught the son the lessons that
he had himself received from his ancestors. He
has made it his glory to bequeath to his successors
the means of securing the greatness of the king-

dom, and the same spirit has thus been maintained for ages. The countries of Europe that preserve their unity have almost-all been peopled by those patient and tenacious races who have preserved and perpetuated the secret of the national thought. A democratic republic does not pursue a similar object. On the contrary, it can scarcely be maintained, except upon condition of setting aside all that recalls the past. Its ideal is different. Its predominant desire is to assure the liberty and equality of mankind. If, unfortunately, that is no longer cherished, it must speedily perish.

It is important for nations who appear to desire a republic not to lose sight of this observation. If, in establishing this form of government, Americans had continued the traditions of the old European *régimes*, they would soon have witnessed its downfall. They were then obliged to accept the essential conditions of their existence. Had they been unable to do so, they would have been reduced to two alternatives—either to establish a monarchy, and clothe the king with considerable power, or to endanger the very life of the nation.

CHAPTER III.

OF FUNCTIONARIES CHARGED WITH ADMINISTRATIVE
ACTION.

" THE administration of government," says the " Federalist," " in its largest sense, comprehends all the operations of the body politic, whether legislative, executive or judicial; but in its most usual, and perhaps in its most precise signification, it is limited to executive details, and falls peculiarly within the province of the executive department. The actual conduct of foreign negotiations, the preparatory plans of finances, the application and disbursement of public moneys in conformity to the general appropriations of the Legislature, the arrangement of the army and navy, the direction of the operations of war. These, and other matters of like nature, constitute what seems to be most properly understood by the administration of government. The persons, therefore, to whose immediate management these different matters are committed, ought to be considered as the assistants or deputies of the chief magistrate, and on this account they ought to derive their offices from his appointment, at least from his nomination, and ought to be subject to his superintendence." [1]

Such were, no doubt, the considerations which controlled the convention in conferring on the President the power of selecting the chiefs of the various departments, who are charged with administrative action.

At the first session of Congress, the question relative to the executive departments was presented. The debates to which their organization gave rise are considered, by competent judges, as the most remarkable, perhaps, which have occurred in the parliamentary history of the United States. The chief point in controversy was as to the power of the President to remove a federal officer. It probably had not specially attracted the attention of the framers of the Constitution. They were aware that he could not be appointed for life, as they made an express exception to this rule in the tenure of office of the members of the supreme and inferior courts. At the same time they declared that the President should, by and with the advice and consent of the Senate, appoint all officers whose appointments were not otherwise provided for in the Constitution, and they authorized Congress to vest the appointment of inferior officers, either in the President, in the courts of law, or in the heads of departments. This clause of the Con-

1 The "Federalist," p. 502.

stitution gave rise to the whole difficulty. A Representative in Congress, who had played an important part in the convention of Philadelphia, insisted that the consent of the Senate was as essential to the removal of an officer as it was to his appointment. Mr. Madison replied that the President had the exclusive power to choose his agents, and that the constitutional restriction touching the intervention of the Senate in appointments should be considered only as an exception, which could not be extended in the absence of an express provision authorizing it. Now there is no clause sanctioning or requiring the action of the Senate in cases of removal. He further contended that the gravest political considerations confirmed this interpretation. "It is," said he, "evidently the intention of the Constitution, that the first magistrate should be responsible for the executive department; so far, therefore, as we do not make the officers who are to aid him in that department responsible to him, he is not responsible to the country." He then pointed out the dangers which would result from the opposite view. The menaced functionary might find supporters in the Senate, and this would give rise to inevitable conflicts between it and the executive." "I believe," said he finally, "that no principle is more clearly established in the Constitution than that of responsibility." Another Representative expressed the same opinions. "If the

President," said he, "complains to the Senate of the misconduct of an officer, and desires their advice and consent to the removal, what are the Senate to do? Naturally they will inquire if the complaint is well founded. To do this, they must call the officer before them to answer. Who, then, are the parties? The supreme executive officer against his assistant, and the Senate are to sit as judges to determine whether sufficient cause for removal exists. Does not this set the Senate over the head of the President? But suppose they shall decide in favor of the officer, what a situation is the President then in, surrounded by officers with whom, by his situation, he is compelled to act, but in whom he can have no confidence." [1]

Such were the considerations that decided the House to recognize the President's constitutional power of removal, at least in all cases where the power to appoint was not subject to legislative delegation.

The Senate had in its turn to pass upon the same question. Mr. Charles Francis Adams thus recounts what took place on this memorable occasion: "But throughout the administration of General Washington there is visible among public men a degree of indifference to power and place, which forms one of the most marked features of that time. To this fact it is owing that public questions of

[1] Debates of Congress, Vol. I., pp. 480-487.

such moment were then discussed with as much personal disinterestedness as can probably ever be expected to enter into them anywhere, yet, even with all these favorable circumstances, it soon became clear that the republican jealousy of a central-ization of power in the President would combine with the *esprit de corps* to rally at least half the Senate in favor of subjecting removals to their control. In such a case the responsibility of deciding the point devolved, by the terms of the Constitution, upon Mr. Adams, as Vice-president. ....It was the first time that he had been summoned to such a duty........His decision settled the question of constitutional power in favor of the President, and consequently established the practice, under the government, which has continued to this day."[1]

In vindicating the action of Congress on the right of removal, Chancellor Kent observes in his commentaries that the power of the President is justified by the most weighty reasons. The subordinate functionaries of the executive department ought to hold at the pleasure of its head, because he is invested generally with the executive authority, and every participation in that authority by the Senate is an exception to a general principle and ought to be taken strictly. "The President is the great functionary, responsible for the faithful execu-

1 Life of John Adams, by Charles Francis Adams, Vol. 1., p. 448.

6

tion of the law, and the power of removal was incidental to that duty, and might often be requisite to fulfill it."[1]

In 1839 the question was also decided in a similar sense by the Supreme Court. Matters rested there until the presidency of Mr. Johnson.

During the session of 1866–67, Congress passed an act "regulating the tenure of certain civil offices." It provides that "every person holding any civil office to which he has been appointed by and with the advice and consent of the Senate, and every person who shall be hereafter appointed to any such office, and shall become duly qualified to act therein, is, and shall be, entitled to hold such office until a successor shall have been in like manner appointed and duly qualified." It adds: "*Provided*, that the Secretaries of State, of the Treasury, of War, of the Navy and the Interior, the Postmaster-general and the Attorney-general, shall hold their offices respectively for and during the term of the President, by whom they may have been appointed."

Mr. Johnson could not mistake the bearing of this measure. It reversed the settled practice of the Government since 1789, and put the President himself under the guardianship of the Senate. At the same time Congress specially had in view keep-

1 Kent's Commentaries, 7th edition, Vol. I., pp. 306–307.
2 Ex-parte Hennen, 13 Peters, p. 139.

ing in office the Secretary of War, in whom the Republican majorities had the utmost confidence, and who, for that very reason, was peculiarly obnoxious to Mr. Johnson. Nevertheless, the latter could not prevent the passage of the bill; it became a law notwithstanding his veto.

A year after the adoption of this measure, which had contributed more than any other to render him powerless, Mr. Johnson thought that he had discovered the means of evading its provisions, and he removed the Secretary of War. The House of Representatives construed this act as a declaration of hostilities.

The long expected occasion occurred, and the President was impeached. It was the province of the Senate, sitting as a high court, for the purpose of trying him, to decide upon his imputed violation of the act of 1867, and also upon the constitutionality of the act itself. The verdict of acquittal proved that, even under the extraordinary circumstances in which it was rendered, the Senate would not so interpret the law as to oblige him to retain in office a hostile Cabinet. The executive thus successfully resisted this exaggerated claim of Congress.

The tenure of office act owed its existence to a peculiar condition of affairs, and to a mistaken belief of its necessity to the safety of the nation. It has been in a great measure repealed, and things have in a great degree returned to their accustomed order. The right of the President to choose the members of the Cabinet, and other administrative functionaries, is no longer subject to any important restrictions.

Aside from some unusual occasions, when party spirit has almost always played a conspicuous part, the President's nominations of the members of his Cabinet have been in general confirmed without difficulty by the Senate. That body has usually respected his wishes, and left him at full liberty to choose his confidential advisers. The practice of the several Presidents has in this respect varied to the greatest extent. Some have appointed to these arduous positions men of distinction, others, personal friends, without experience or special qualifications. Washington called to his aid two of the most eminent statesmen of the day, and exerted all his influence to bring about their harmonious co-operation. In our times, Mr. Lincoln selected his council from the leaders of the Republican party, among whom were Mr. Seward and Mr. Chase.

The last Cabinet of General Jackson, on the contrary, was chiefly composed of his obsequious instruments. They were not brought to his notice by their prominent position before the country. Their principal title to his recognition was an attachment to his person and an unhesitating support of his cause. But never, perhaps, was the system

then inaugurated pushed so far as under the presidency of General Grant. With the exception of
two or three, whose appointment may have met
the wishes of the party which elected him, the
members of his Cabinet owed their elevation to
personal favor alone. Whatever may, in other
respects, be thought of this practice, it seems to be
a plain violation of the spirit, if not the letter, of
the Constitution. The President ought to be surrounded by able and experienced men, capable of
sharing with him the labors of the government.
The Constitution provides that "he may require
the opinion in writing of the principal officer in
each of the executive departments upon any subject relating to the duties of their respective offices."
This clause can only be fully carried out by selecting such officers from among the most eminent
statesmen; for when the complicated and arduous
duties devolving upon them are considered, simply
personal friends cannot meet its requirements.

The practice upon another point is far from uniform. The President is not bound to ask the
opinion of his advisers upon all pending questions.
He may either take their individual views, or call
them together for consultation; but in case their
united opinions are contrary to his own, he is not
obliged to conform to them. In such a case, the
secretaries would doubtless be justified in tendering
their resignations; yet the rules of American pub-

lic life do not make such an extreme course imperative. They may, if they so prefer, submit to his
will and quietly retain their portfolios.

In general, important Cabinet deliberations are
confidential. It is therefore very difficult to ascertain exactly the relations of the President with his
secretaries. Nevertheless, aided by disclosures that
time brings about, discoveries are occasionally made
of the manner of deciding great measures.

Thus, from different documents relating to the
presidency of Washington, we learn how, at that
period, business was transacted between him and
his Cabinet. Such, for example, is John Marshall's
account of the deliberations when the neutrality
policy of the United States was determined. France
had just declared war against the English and the
Dutch. What attitude ought the United States to
assume? A question of the gravest import. The
President wrote immediately to Thomas Jefferson,
Secretary of State: "War having actually commenced between France and Great Britain, it be-
hooves the government of this country to use all the
means in its power to prevent the citizens thereof
from embroiling us with either of these powers,
by endeavoring to maintain a strict neutrality. I,
therefore, require that you will give the subject
mature consideration, that such measures as shall
be deemed most likely to effect this desirable
purpose may be adopted without delay........."

Some days later, the President addressed to the members of his Cabinet a circular letter submitting thirteen questions. They met and upon certain points were unanimous, but upon others they could not agree. He then requested a written opinion from each of them. Based upon these documents, he established that foreign policy which is still maintained by the United States.[1]

During the progress of the war of secession Mr. Lincoln followed a very different practice. Notwithstanding the portentous gravity of the situation, it seems that he very seldom called a Cabinet meeting, with a view of asking advice. It is probable, for instance, that without previously consulting them upon its expediency, he read to his Cabinet the emancipation proclamation of 22d of September, 1862, which embodied and gave effect to his own deliberate views and purposes upon that momentous question. It is generally thought that he pursued the same course with regard to the second proclamation of emancipation, bearing date 1st January, 1863. It appears that, when he communicated it to his Cabinet, the Secretary of the Treasury, Mr. Chase, suggested that it ought to contain some sentence less technical than the others, and presenting at least a moral consideration or reflection. Mr. Lincoln proposed to Mr. Chase to prepare it,

1Life of George Washington, by John Marshall, Vol. V., pp. 401-404.

which he did, by inserting the concluding words of that memorable document: "And upon this act, sincerely believed to be an act of justice, warranted by the Constitution upon military necessity, I invoke the considerate judgment of mankind and the gracious favor of Almighty God." The part taken by Mr. Lincoln's advisers in one of the most important decisions of the age, seems to have been limited to drawing up this felicitous expression.

At the very moment when the armies of the Union triumphed on all sides, a question, almost as weighty as that of emancipation, was forced upon the attention of Mr. Lincoln. It was necessary to determine the policy to be adopted with regard to the States lately in rebellion. Mr. Stanton, one of the most distinguished members of the Cabinet, thus related before a congressional committee of inquiry what took place on this occasion : "Shortly previous to that time I had myself, with a view of putting in a practicable form the means of overcoming what seemed to be a difficulty in the mind of Mr. Lincoln as to the mode of reconstruction, prepared a rough draft of a form or mode by which the authority and laws of the United States should be re-established.........In the course of that consultation Mr. Lincoln alluded to the paper, went into his room, brought it out, and asked me to read it, which I did, and explained my ideas in regard to it.........." I was requested by the other members of the Cabinet, and by Mr. Lincoln, to have a copy printed for each member for subsequent consideration........That night Mr. Lincoln was murdered. Subsequently, at an early day, the subject came under consideration, after the surrender of Johnston's army, in the Cabinet of Mr. Johnson. The *project* I had prepared was printed, and a copy placed in the hands of each member of the Cabinet and the President. It was somewhat altered in some particulars, and came under discussion in the Cabinet, the principal point of discussion being as to who should exercise the elective franchise. I think there was a difference of opinion in the Cabinet upon that subject. The President expressed his views very clearly and distinctly. I expressed my views, and other members of the Cabinet expressed their views. The objections of the President to throwing the franchise open to the colored people appeared to be fixed, and I think every member of the Cabinet assented to the arrangement as it was specified in the proclamation relative to North Carolina.[1] After that I do not remember that the subject was ever again discussed in the Cabinet."[2]

[1] It is this proclamation that determines the conditions under which the Southern States were to be re-admitted into the Union. It is known that at a later period Congress refused to approve of this plan of *reconstruction.*

[2] Impeachment Investigation, 2d Session, 39th Congress, and 1st Session 40th Congress, 1867, p. 401.

We must here inquire how far a decision of the Cabinet would, under certain contingencies, tend to shield the President from responsibility. Very different answers have been made to this question. A distinction can moreover be established. If his political responsibility is in question, it is evidently, under the Constitution, devolved exclusively upon him. Had a unanimous written opinion on any measure been obtained from his Cabinet, still the people would none the less consider him as the only author of it.

Is it, on the contrary, a question of criminal liability? It is certain that a President, impeached for an act suggested or explicitly approved by his Cabinet, can always plead his good faith in the premises. Let us suppose, for instance, that the interpretation of a law is involved, and that the Attorney-general, to whom it was submitted, gave a written opinion, in which all the secretaries concurred.. The President can always allege that he with good motives and for justifiable ends acted in conformity with this opinion, although it is of questionable soundness. Thus, the action of the Cabinet may in certain cases, and to a limited extent, relieve the President from the penal consequences of an act not palpably in violation of the law of the land.

Such is the organization of the different branches of the public service which constitute the executive department. The chief magistrate confides the supervision of them to the men of his choice. If they are prominent members of his party, he must neglect nothing to secure their friendly and efficient co-operation. Among them there may be several presidential aspirants, and one of the principal difficulties with which he may have to contend may arise from this source, springing up in the very bosom of his administration. He must then judge on what conditions these rival candidates, who are in such close official relations with him, can be prevailed on to subordinate to the public interests their ambitious personal aims.

Undoubtedly the President, by inviting to his Cabinet obscure personal friends, will avoid this danger. He must, in that event, be a superior, self-relying man, conscious of his power to master at all times the political situation; but even then the selection of novices for advisers is an experiment full of danger. He should therefore avoid it, and yet the history of the United States furnishes numerous precedents, which will scarcely encourage him to call around him noted political personages. On almost every page will be found traces of those internal strifes which divided the Cabinets of his predecessors. Very often intrigues have been prompted by the desire of the occupants of the most important posts to gain an exceptional place, by which they may attract the attention, and ultimately se-

cure the suffrages of the people. As the term is
only for a limited period, all citizens having elevated positions may aspire to the chief magistracy.
Thus restless ambition is ever at work and every
possible candidate on the alert. Hence unnumbered
rivalries, and never-ceasing combinations, which
embarrass the President and paralyze his power.
In his own Cabinet are often his most dangerous
adversaries, and it requires all his skill and patience
to submit to this state of things, which, it seems,
exist in all countries, where the republican system
prevails.

The experience of a republic, already acquired by
the United States, permits us at least to point out
the defects inherent in the elective system as applied
to the chief magistracy. It must be admitted that
they are not so sensibly felt in the constitution of
the legislative and judicial branches of the government, and that the questions relating to them
were solved in quite a satisfactory manner by the
convention of 1787. In organizing the executive,
that body had often to run counter to the very nature
of things, and could do no better, for in that department are found the defects in the republican system,
for which no efficient remedy has yet been, or can
be devised.

It was necessary to confer on the President very
extensive powers and to forbid the people abridging
their duration, and at the same time to avoid the

formation of a Cabinet depending for its existence upon the pleasure of Congress. How were these propositions to be reconciled with the principles of political responsibility. It must then be sacrificed or its application rendered illusory. It was impossible for the Legislature to avoid creating different executive departments, and it was still more impossible to withdraw them from the exclusive control of the President. He must therefore put at the head of them men of weight and influence in the country, who, in most instances, will aspire to succeed him, and who will very often embarrass his administration; or he can select his personal friends, and, in that event, he will form merely a corps of clerks, but in no just sense a Cabinet.

Those nations who aspire to a republican government should carefully reflect upon these problems, which have not been hitherto solved. If, as everything leads us to believe, they are unable to give them a satisfactory solution, they should submit to the inconveniences inseparable from an elective *régime.* There is scarcely an intelligent man in the United States who does not feel them, and yet everybody accepts them—an example of wisdom which, for more than eighty years, has been given by the American people to those nations who desire to tread in their footsteps.

CHAPTER IV.

RELATIONS OF THE PRESIDENT TO CONGRESS.

ALTHOUGH, as we have seen, neither the President nor the principal executive agents are politically amenable to Congress, nevertheless, as one of the " co-ordinate " branches of the government, he has constant relations with each of the others, especially the legislative.

In taking into view these relations it must not be forgotten that the political party which elects the President has almost always been able to command a majority in the House of Representatives of the first Congress which meets after his inauguration. Matters are much more complicated in regard to the Senate. As it is a permanent body, of which one-third of the members are biennially chosen, more than that number cannot, during the year of the presidential election, be secured in any way by the dominant party. So decisive a result is, indeed, very rarely attained, as it requires a majority in the Legislature of each State in whose senatorial delegation there is a vacancy to be filled. A party must, therefore, be in the ascendency for many years in the country to obtain a majority in the Senate. That body seldom makes such factious opposition as will arrest the action of the government, if the lower house concurs with the President in his views of public policy. Should he, however, have cause to expect resistance in both houses, he has none the less a right to propose to them such legislation as he deems to be wise and just.

As a matter of fact, the order of things is this: "The President," says the Constitution, "shall from time to time give to Congress information of the state of the Union, and recommend to their consideration such measures as he shall judge necessary and expedient." In performing the duty thus enjoined, he sends to Congress each year, at the opening of the session, a message containing as well a complete exposition of his policy, as a statement of the condition of affairs, and suggesting such action as the public service seems to require. It is accompanied by special reports of almost all the secretaries, who recommend in general the passage of certain laws, and transmit, in support of their opinion, an immense mass of documents, so arranged as to fully exhibit all the details of the administration. These various reports are intended to furnish a complete summary of the situation. The first question that arises, then, is whether Congress will adopt the measures thus submitted to it.

These communications are soon followed by

others.[1] Let us take, for example, those which relate to the funds required for carrying on the government. The documents on the subject are prepared by the executive departments and submitted to the House. As the appropriation bills contain from eight to nine hundred items, it is very natural that the members of the committee charged with the duty of preparing them should consider it indispensable for them to be fully informed. They hold frequent conferences with the different secretaries, and the latter furnish the requested explanations, sometimes by writing, but in most instances orally, as special inquiries are made. Sometimes the chiefs of bureaus perform this office. The money bills are the result of this long and elaborate examination and interchange of views. It will thus be seen that, although the administration is not officially represented in the public debates, it participates with none the less activity in the preliminary preparations. It is only after a mutual agreement between the members of the Cabinet and the House committee, that the latter report the bills which have been prepared after a severe scrutiny and by their common consent. When the House passes them, they are sent to the Senate, and there referred in turn to the appropriate committee or committees. If the administration is not satisfied

1 If Congress is organized, the budget is sometimes laid before the appropriate committee, who meet *ad hoc* even before the beginning of the session.

with the sums granted by the House, it may en-
deavor to get an increase from the Senate. Here,
also, it is at liberty to have its views presented,
and things take very much the same course as they
did before the House.

What has just been stated with regard to the
budget applies to almost all laws and joint resolutions discussed during the session. If the President
at any time thinks that Congress ought to adopt a
measure, he can send a special message recom-
mending it. On the contrary, when Congress takes
the initiative in any matters which may affect his
administration, he has the right to present his
opinion before the committee to which they have
been referred, and if it is not heeded, he may invite
his friends to attack the measure, and to say that
he disapproves it. In that case it is almost always
made a party question; involving either the defeat
or the success of the administration. If he prefers
to employ other means, he is at liberty to do so;
he may, for example, invite Senators and Representatives to confer with him. He may, also,
instruct a member of his Cabinet, to draw up a bill,
and put it in the hands of a member of either House,
who will introduce it in his own name. In such
case, the true author of the measure will be generally
known or at least suspected. Those who are
conversant with the legislation of past years can

7

mention many important laws prepared and drawn up by one of the secretaries.

The relations between the President and Congress are also affected by the composition of his Cabinet. In the latter are frequently found several prominent ex-members of the Senate or House. These parliamentary leaders, in withdrawing from Congress, maintain their personal, and, to a certain degree, even their political relations with their former colleagues. Secretaries have often in this way continued to direct the political party to which they belong. But if, as he is permitted to do, the President prefers to isolate himself from Congress, and selects his counselors from dependents and personal friends who have never played an important part in politics, then his means of influence will be greatly diminished; and it may happen that Congress will emancipate itself from administrative influence. We have so far assumed that the friends and supporters of the President have a majority in Congress; should they on the contrary be in a minority in one or both Houses, his opponents will then limit themselves for the most part to thwarting his action; and some conflicts may even break forth. But the Constitution co-ordinates the two powers in such manner that the people will soon be called upon for their decision. However, before affairs proceed to this extremity, he is clothed with a power which may be always exercised in case Congress pass such bills as he considers to be unconstitutional or dangerous.

By the terms of the Constitution, "Every bill which shall have passed the House of Representatives and the Senate shall, before it becomes a law, be presented to the President of the United States; if he approve, he shall sign it; but if not, he shall return it, with his objections, to that House in which it shall have originated, who shall enter the objections at large on their journal, and proceed to reconsider it. If, after such reconsideration, two-thirds of that House shall agree to pass the bill, it shall be sent, together with the objections, to the other House, by which it shall likewise be considered, and, if approved by two-thirds of that House, it shall become a law. But in all such cases the votes of both Houses shall be determined by yeas and nays; and the names of the persons voting for and against the bill shall be entered on the journal of each House respectively. If any bill shall not be returned by the President, within ten days (Sundays excepted) after it shall have been presented to him, the same shall be a law in like manner as if he had signed it, unless the Congress, by their adjournment, prevent its return, in which case it shall not be a law."

"Every order, resolution, or vote, to which the concurrence of the Senate and House of Representatives may be necessary (except on a question of adjournment), shall be presented to the President of the United States.........."[1]

Thus he is placed under one of the following alternatives: he either signs a bill, in which case it becomes a law, or he withholds his approval and returns the bill, or joint resolution, to the House in which it originated, with a message setting forth his objections. If Congress persists, then a second vote, requiring a two-thirds majority of each House to be effectual, must be taken. Finally, if he does not fully approve a legislative act, and at the same time does not think it requisite so to return it, he may refrain from either course, and then, after the lapse of ten days, it will become a law. But if it is presented to him toward the close of the session, so that he has not the full period for considering it given by the Constitution, then his non-concurrence is fatal to its validity. He may also sign it under protest. Several instances of this kind are recorded in the legislative history of the United States.

It is proper to remark, that the separate action of one of the legislative branches may morally influence the President, but it has no legal force or effect. He is left at liberty to be guided by this expression of opinion, or to proceed in such course as he may have adopted. In the session of 1863-64, for example, the House of Representatives

[1] Constitution, Article 1., Section 7.

unanimously adopted a resolution protesting against the establishment of an empire in Mexico, in favor of an Austrian prince. The Senate, with the view of suppressing the question, abstained from discussing that resolution. The French authorities were none the less roused, and requested an explanation of it. The Secretary of State replied by disavowing any responsibility therefor on the part of the government, and said that a vote of the House of Representatives or of the Senate could neither coerce the executive to modify its policy, nor deprive it of freedom of action. This matter, in the course of December, 1864, came before the House of Representatives. By an immense majority they affirmed their right to advise on questions of foreign policy; but this declaration does not appear to have had any influence on the course of the administration.

The motives which determined the framers of the Constitution to confer on the executive so large a legislative authority, are explained in the following manner by the authors of the "Federalist:" "The propensity of the legislative department to intrude upon the rights, and to absorb the powers of the other departments, has been already suggested and repeated; the insufficiency of a mere parchment delineation of the boundaries of each has also been remarked upon; and the necessity of furnishing each with constitutional arms for its own defense has been inferred and proved. From these clear and indubitable principles, results the propriety of a negative, either absolute or qualified, in the executive, upon the acts of the legislative branches. Without the one or the other the former would be absolutely unable to defend himself against the depredations of the latter. He might gradually be stripped of his authority by successive resolutions, or annihilated by a single vote. And in the one mode or the other the legislative and executive powers might speedily come to be blended in the same hands, if even no propensity had ever discovered itself in the legislative body to invade the rights of the executive! The power not only serves as a shield to the executive, but it furnishes an additional security against the enaction of improper laws. It establishes a salutary check upon the legislative body calculated to guard the community against the effects of faction. The propriety of a negative has, upon some occasions, been combatted by an observation that it was not to be presumed a single man would possess more virtue and wisdom than a number of men, and that unless this presumption should be entertained, it would be improper to give the executive magistrate any species of control over the legislative body. The primary inducement to conferring the power in question upon the executive is to enable him to defend himself; the secondary one is to increase the chances in favor of the community against the passing of bad laws through haste, inadvertence or design. Nor is this all. The superior weight and influence of the legislative body in a free government, and the hazard to the executive in trial of strength with that body, afford a satisfactory security that the negative would generally be employed with great caution, and there would the oftener be room for a charge of timidity than of rashness in the exercise of it. But the Convention has pursued a mean in this business which will both facilitate the exercise of the power vested in this respect in the executive magistrate, and make its efficacy to depend on the sense of a considerable part of the legislative body. Instead of an absolute negative, it is proposed to give the executive the qualified negative already described. This is a power which would be more readily exercised than the other. A man who might be afraid to defeat a law by his single *veto* might not scruple to return it for reconsideration.........He would be encouraged by the reflection that, if his opposition should prevail, it would embark in it a very respectable proportion of the legislative body, whose influence would be united with his in supporting the propriety of his conduct in the public opinion."[1]

The considerations which decided the framers of the Constitution to adopt the compromise of a quali-

---

[1] The "Federalist," p. 510 *et. seq.*

fied negative were for the most part just and sound;
however, after an experience of nearly a century,
the situation has undergone considerable change.

Although the veto power is indispensable to the
maintenance of the executive prerogatives, it is
now evident that its exercise may lead to fierce
antagonisms full of disaster to the country, were it
not for the frequent recurrence of elections, by
which the people, the ultimate source of power,
can decide the matters in controversy.

The 10th July, 1832, President Jackson returned
to the Senate the bill re-chartering the Bank of the
United States. Without here entering on the details of this affair, in which the most violent passions of both parties were enlisted, it suffices to
say that he, the acknowledged head of the Democratic party, was, on this occasion, in opposition to
the Whigs, then led by Mr. Webster and Mr. Clay,
and commanding a considerable majority in the
Senate. In his memorable veto message the President said:

"The Congress, the executive and the court
must each for itself be guided by its own opinion
of the Constitution. Each public officer, who takes
an oath to support the Constitution, swears that he
will support it as he understands it and not as it is
understood by others. It is as much the duty of
the House of Representatives, of the Senate and
of the President to decide upon the constitutionality

of any bill or resolution which may be presented
to them for passage or approval, as it is of the supreme judges, when it may be brought before them
for judicial decision. The opinion of the judges
has no more authority over Congress than the opinion of Congress has over the judges, and on that
point the President is independent of both."[1]

These propositions could not be seriously controverted by the Whig leaders. All their skill was
exerted in shaping the issues to be presented to the
people at the then approaching election. They
knew that in the then condition of parties it was
impossible to carry the measure over the veto;
but they relied upon a favorable verdict from that
sovereign power whose decision in the last resort
was about to be invoked. They were deceived in
their expectations. In the following November
the President was re-elected by an overwhelming
majority.

From the administration of General Jackson to
that of Mr. Johnson several Presidents exercised
the veto power, and with but one exception the
measures thus returned to Congress could not be
passed a second time.

Under Mr. Johnson affairs assumed a different
aspect; but we must note how very peculiar

1 See Thirty Years' View, Vol. I., p. 251 *et seq.* See also the message accompanying the President's veto, in Presidents' Messages,
p. 418 *et seq.*

was the then existing situation, and not ascribe
undue importance to the occurrences of his administration, nor draw too positive conclusions from
them.   Certainly, if a Vice-president, suddenly
placed at the head of the government, was satisfied
with the simple fulfillment of his duties, without
attempting to impress his peculiar views upon the
public mind or control the political action of the
country, he would probably avoid angry controversies.   But this was not the case with Mr. Johnson.
An obstinate will, a very narrow intellect, and
perhaps also the violence of ardent convictions,
prompted him, in the crisis through which the
country was passing, to assume an attitude well
fitted to excite resentment and opposition.   Congress had compact Republican majorities, with
skillful and determined leaders.   Under such
circumstances a struggle was inevitable.   So Congress had not been in session one hour before
the quarrel commenced (first Monday of December, 1865); and it continued, without intermission,
until March 4th, 1869, when he was succeeded by
Grant.   During that time he vetoed all the political
measures of Congress, and the latter almost always
passed them the second time, notwithstanding his
opposition.   However, it must not be thought that,
under these altogether exceptional circumstances,
the majority in each House were free from doubt
or acted without hesitation.   The first veto of Mr.

Johnson was sustained by the Senate, to which he had transmitted the message giving his objections. Some weeks later he pursued the same course with regard to another bill, when a violent contest took place in the Senate, which was prolonged through many sessions. Up to the last moment the result of the vote was uncertain, and it was with great difficulty that the Republican party could unite the requisite majority of two-thirds. But this bill, having been passed over the veto, the decisive step was taken. Then, in the name of the public welfare, it was, in the opinion of Congress, expedient and necessary to restrain the power of the President by legislative acts.

It might be supposed that by reason of these conflicts the Constitution would be modified, the independence of the executive permanently affected, and the legislative authority rendered supreme. Such were in effect the consequences involved when the House of Representatives impeached the President, and sent him before the Senate for trial.

In another part of this work will be found an analysis of the principal points raised by this trial, but it must be here remarked how, on this solemn occasion, the counsel of Mr. Johnson claimed in his name the right to interpret the sense and determine the scope of a statute. They argued that, charged with the faithful execution of the laws, he could not perform this arduous duty otherwise than by a vigilant supervision of the subordinate officers, by whose instrumentality he acted. In the attainment of this end he must exercise the right of interpretation. Now, if he is doubtful as to the meaning of any provision, he has then the privilege of taking the advice of the members of his Cabinet. His constitutional oath obliges him not only to execute the laws, but also to support the Constitution itself, and this great trust implies the exercise of a large discretion. This doctrine, added one of the ablest advocates of Mr. Johnson, has been sustained by the decisions of the Supreme Court, affirming that, in the administration of the laws, the President was not a simple ministerial officer, but that he exercised executive and political functions. He had then a certain freedom of action that Congress could not rightfully restrain.[1] This opinion is constitutional. The acquittal of President Johnson soon proved that, even in extreme cases, the Legislature should confine its attacks within the certain limits ordained by the Constitution.

Moreover, the contest could not be carried further; and in fact, at the very time when the Senate decided the fate of Mr. Johnson, the Republican National Convention met at Chicago, and nominated General Grant for the presidency. Without openly disavowing the policy which had led Congress to impeach Mr. Johnson, the Republican

[1] Impeachment Trial, Mr. Stanberry's argument, pp. 773-74.

party showed by its attitude that matters could not be pushed to the last extremity. A reaction in the country was manifestly taking place. The people were about to appear on the scene, and in their turn judge the judges. As might have been expected, when the nation called General Grant to preside over its destinies, the natural balance of powers was re-established. After his inauguration he regained, in a few months, almost as a matter of course, nearly all the ground lost by his predecessor. At the present day the presidential authority is perhaps relatively stronger than when General Jackson left office.

Thus the American Executive Power has been able to sustain itself throughout the most critical periods, and, aside from the occasional instances when the Vice-president exercised its functions, has triumphed in every contest between it and Congress.

And it is well here to observe, that the frequency of elections always permits the masses to intervene seasonably and to proclaim their will. It may be thought dangerous, perhaps, to remit to them the final judgment of such delicate questions. In the United States, however, the verdicts of the nation are in general sound and prudent. The public conscience is not deadened or perverted by party spirit. The people calmly investigate and wisely determine. In a republic the soverignty must be effectively exercised by them. Congress and the President himself are to be considered as their delegates, and, in a certain sense, their agents, or, as General Grant expressed it in one of his happiest inspirations, "This country is a republic, where the will of the people must be obeyed."

If the presidential term were prolonged two years the nation would not be deprived of the right to express its opinion. In fact the House of Representatives would continue to be integrally renewed as it has been, and the Senate would become entirely so, during this period of six years. The people could express their approval or disapproval, by sending to the House or the Senate friends or opponents of the policy of the President, and at the same time the local elections enable them to declare their opinions, which, if he is wise, he will carefully heed.

It has now been shown in what way the Executive Power "forms a co-ordinate branch of the government," how, as such, it intervenes in legislative questions, and how its action is felt in all the phases through which a bill or resolution must pass in order to become eventually a law. It remains to be seen why the President is independent of Congress.

We must, in the first place, observe that, except by way of *impeachment*, the legislative power has no constitutional means of reaching the President.

One of the most distinguished members of the
Philadelphia convention, Roger Sherman, advocated
in that assembly the theory that the executive
magistracy should be instituted for the sole purpose
of doing the behests of the Legislature; that it should
be, elected by and be responsible to, Congress—in a
word, that the latter ought to be the representative
and exponent of the supreme will of the country.
He therefore proposed that it should be vested with
the power of organizing the executive in the manner which it might deem the most advantageous.[1]
But, as we have seen, this opinion found no favor
in the convention. It decided that the President
should be independent of the Legislature. The latter,
then, cannot in reality attack this independence without violating the Constitution, and if it hesitated to go
that far, it would speedily feel its own impotency.

This question was first presented at the moment
of General Jackson's re-election by an immense
majority. Although this re-election had notably
affected the composition of the House of Representatives, the Whigs still had a majority in the Senate, and they also found allies in Senator Calhoun
and his personal friends. Thus the violent contest, commenced under the first administration of
General Jackson, was continued after his re-election. It then assumed a new phase. Mr. Clay,
the leader of the coalition, taking advantage of a

[1] The Madison Papers, Vol. II., p. 763.

supposed favorable circumstance, offered in the Senate a resolution censuring the President, which, after long debates, was adopted by a vote of 26 to 20. General Jackson answered by protesting. This rigid defender of the Executive Power thus proved that this high assembly had exceeded its rightful authority.

"That the Senate," said he, " possesses a high judicial power, and that instances may occur in which the President of the United States will be amenable to it, is undeniable. But under the provisions of the Constitution it would seem to be equally plain that neither the President nor any other officer can be rightfully subjected to the operation of the judicial power of the Senate, except in the cases and under the forms prescribed by the Constitution. The Constitution declares that the President, Vice-president, and all civil officers of the United States, shall be removed from office on impeachment for and conviction of treason, bribery, and other high crimes and misdemeanors. That the House of Representatives shall have the sole power of impeachment. That the Senate 'shall have the sole power to try all impeachments.' That, 'when sitting for that purpose, they shall be on oath or affirmation.' That 'when the President of the United States is tried, the Chief Justice shall preside.' That 'no person shall be convicted without the concurrence of two-thirds of the members present..........'

" The resolution above quoted," continues General Jackson, " charges in substance that in certain proceedings relating to the public revenue the President has usurped authority and power not conferred upon him by the Constitution and laws, and that in doing so he violated both. Any such act constitutes a high crime—one of the highest indeed which the President can commit—a crime which justly exposes him to impeachment by the House of Representatives, and upon due conviction to removal from office."

But even admitting the Senate's right to pass this vote of censure, it could do nothing more. It had no means of forcing the President in his stronghold. It was therefore constrained to confine its further action to a refusal to receive his protest in answer. On the other hand his friends at once went to work. The Senator who particularly represented the ideas of the administration, immediately announced that he should propose not only . to rescind the resolution, but even to expunge it from the journal. To this end he soon after made a motion in due form. It was, of course, at first rejected by the same majority that had adopted the resolution; but the popular reaction in favor of General Jackson continued to increase, and at the succeeding partial renewal of the Senate a

8

majority of the members elected were found to be
devoted to him.   Finally, three years after he
had been censured, the expunging resolution was
adopted.   At that moment a Senator rose and said,
that it only remained to execute at once the order
of the Senate.

"The Secretary thereupon produced the original
manuscript journal of the Senate, and opening at
the page which contained the condemnatory sentence of March 28th, 1834, proceeded in open Senate to draw a square of broad black lines around
the sentence, and to write across its face in strong
letters these words: 'Expunged by order of the
Senate, this 16th day of March, 1837.'"[1]

Thus General Jackson came victorious out of
this struggle.   Without pronouncing a judgment
upon his character, which cannot yet be done with
entire impartiality, it suffices to remark that during his two terms the Executive Power was maintained in its plentitude, and that he achieved this
signal success by his energy in defending his constitutional prerogatives.

Since then Congress has had many contests with
the President.   It has not in the main gained more
over him, than he has over it.   In fact, that branch
of the Government which seeks to attack the other
cannot do so, in the greater number of instances,
without exceeding the limits of the Constitution.

[1] Thirty Years' View, Vol. I., p. 730.

The framers of the Constitution so effectually guarded the independence of the executive, that Congress has not been able to deal it fatal blows. Upon the whole, the prerogatives of the President are to day nearly what they were in the time of Washington; they have even been rather increased than diminished.

.The "Federalist" observed that the legislative power always tended to intrench upon the other branches of the government, and it feared that the President could not resist its attacks. These fears were ill-founded; at least the danger was exaggerated. Elected by the people, the first magistrate of the republic sways the popular mind with that natural ascendency which a living and acting personality exercises over the masses. They behold in him their direct representative. Congress, on the contrary, appears to them as a kind of abstraction, and in a contest their instincts lead them to sustain him. It must, then, be under very exceptional conditions that they will do violence to their inclinations and give their support to Congress when opposed to him.

CHAPTER V.

WE cannot here refrain from presenting some considerations on the province assigned by the Constitution to the Legislative and the Executive Power in questions concerning peace and war.

At their session, August 17th, 1787, the convention discussed, for the first time, that portion of the draft of the Constitution in which this grave problem was placed. The most contradictory opinions were in turn advanced. It was proposed to confer on the Legislature the power "to *make* war." Two members of the convention asked that the word "*declare*" should be substituted for "*make*"; for in this way, said. they, the executive would be in a position to repel any sudden attack.

This motion having been adopted by an almost unanimous vote, it followed that the power of declaring war was confided to the legislature, whilst the convention remitted to the President and Senate that of making peace.[1] The temper of

1 The Madison Papers, Vol. III., p. 1551 *et. seq.*

the convention was eminently pacific, and opposed to invasion and conquest. As was said in debate, the members of that assembly desired to make it more difficult to declare war than to conclude a treaty of peace.

In commenting upon these constitutional provisions, the Supreme Court of the United States· has expressed itself in the following manner:

"But the genius and character of our institutions are peaceful, and the power to declare war was not conferred upon Congress for the purposes of aggression or aggrandizement, but to enable the general government to vindicate, by arms, if it should become necessary, its own rights and the rights of its citizens."

"A war, therefore, declared by Congress, can never be presumed to be waged for the purpose of conquest or the acquisition of territory."[2]

At the same time that the convention gave to the legislature the war-declaring power, it chose to reserve to the President the duty of repelling all attacks which might come either from abroad or at home; it also wished to enable him to act without delay, a precaution worthy of praise, the wisdom of which was justified by the events of the Spring of 1861. This contingency occurred at the moment when Fort Sumter fell into the hands of the insurgent forces. President

2 See Heming *vs.* Page, 9 Howard, p. 614.

Lincoln, without loss of time, issued his proclamation, April 16, 1861, calling forth the militia of the several States to the aggregate number of 75,000, and convening an extraordinary session of Congress. Four days later, 19th April following, he declared the blockade of the southern ports. Thus the power of declaring war, of summoning the militia to arms, and of blockading ports, which the Constitution appeared to grant to Congress alone, was exercised by him.

At first sight, nothing would seem more illegal, and yet, not only did Congress ratify the action of the President, but the Supreme Court also explained, in an important decision, why he, in thus taking the initiative, had only exercised the power conferred upon him.

" As a civil war," said the Supreme Court, "is never publicly proclaimed, *eo nomine*, against insurgents, its actual existence is a fact in our domestic history which the court is bound to notice and to know."

" The true tests of its existence are found in the writings of the sages of the common law, and may be thus summarily stated: 'When the regular course of justice is interrupted by revolt, rebellion, or insurrection, so that the courts of justice cannot be kept open, *civil war exists*, and hostilities may be prosecuted on the same footing as if those opposing

the government were foreign enemies invading the
land.'"

"By the Constitution," adds the Supreme Court,
"Congress alone has the power to declare a national
or foreign war. It cannot declare war against a
State, or any number of States, by virtue of any
clause in the Constitution. The Constitution confers
on the President the whole Executive Power. He
is bound to take care that the laws be faithfully
executed. He is commander-in-chief of the army
and navy of the United States, and of the militia
of the several States when called into the actual service of the United States. He has no power to
initiate or declare a war either against a foreign
nation or a domestic State. But by the acts of
Congress of February 28th, 1795, and March 3d,
1807, he is authorized to call out the militia and
use the military and naval forces of the United
States in case of invasion by foreign nations, and to
suppress insurrection against the government of a
State or of the United States."

"If a war be made by invasion of a foreign nation the President is not only authorized but bound
to resist force by force. He does not initiate the
war, but is bound to accept the challenge without
waiting for any special legislative authority. And
whether the hostile party be a foreign invader, or
States organized in rebellion, it is none the less a
war, although the declaration of it be 'unilate-

ral.'" Lord Stowell observes: "It is not the less a war on that account, for war may exist without a declaration on either side. It is so laid down by the best writers on the law of nations. A declaration of war by one country only is not a mere challenge to be accepted or refused at pleasure by one country only".........and further on, the Supreme Court, continuing the same argument, says: "If it were necessary to the technical existence of a war that it should have a legislative sanction, we find it in almost every act passed at the extraordinary session of the Legislature of 1861 ....Without admitting that such an act was necessary under the circumstances, it is plain that if the President had in any manner assumed powers which it was necessary should have the authority or sanction of Congress ....this ratification has operated to perfectly cure the defect.........We are of opinion that the President had a right, *jure belli*, to institute a blockade of ports in possession of the States in rebellion."[1]

The doctrine announced by the Supreme Court may, then, be summed up as follows: The Legislature has the power to declare war, but it should never be aggressive; the United States should limit itself to the defensive, and cause the rights

[1] Claimants of Schooners Brillant, Crushaw, Bark Hiawatha and others,.*vs.* The United States, 9th March, 1869. Black's Reports, Vol. II., pp. 665 *et seq.*

of American citizens to be respected abroad; and, on the other hand, if the Union is attacked, the President should take all necessary measures to defend the country.

When the framers of the Constitution vested in Congress exclusively the power to declare war, their thought might seem to be as just as their intentions were wise. They appeared to foresee the terrible influence of that "spirit of conquest and usurpation" which was about to break forth in Europe with unexampled violence. Opposed as they were to aggressive war, they used many precautions to forestall its fatal consequences. However, when the means to which they had recourse are considered, we may question if they were not laboring under illusions. In fact, according to the terms of the judicial decision just cited, a President who conducts affairs with a foreign power, so as skillfully to lead it to attack the United States, can always engage the action of the country and inaugurate defensive war.

If the American republic has, in the course of its history, almost constantly manifested a pacific disposition, it cannot be attributed to the constitutional article relating to the war-power. The progress of this work will show how a foreign policy was established in the United States calculated to moderate a spirit of aggression. But the credit of having inaugurated and maintained it is principally due to the Presidents, and it is at least doubtful if Congress would have evinced similar wisdom. However that may be, it is important to remark the interpretation given by the Supreme Court and by Congress itself to the constitutional clause in question. On the President is enjoined the high duty of watching over the maintenance of the Union. He will, therefore, repell foreign invasion and suppress domestic insurrection without awaiting the instructions of Congress. In a word, his remaining on the defensive is all that is required to authorize him to act. Possessing such powers, a President, animated with a war-like spirit, is always able to initiate hostilities. In studying the diplomacy of other nations, it would not be difficult for him to find numerous precedents, and to learn the art of inviting an attack, when, in reality, he would be the aggressor. The issue once made, the honor of the nation once at stake, patriotic sentiments would be excited in the United States probably sooner than elsewhere, and the constitutional guaranty, which intrusts to the Legislature exclusively the power of declaring war, would thus become an empty phrase, signifying nothing.

We thus perceive that the President has, in most all questions of foreign policy, a very large control. The Constitution attempted, without doubt, to restrict it within narrower limits: but custom

has constrained legislators as well as judges to give
to these clauses an interpretation generally favorable
to his authority. The latter has been augmented
and confirmed by the trials to which it has been
subjected. Ought the United States to regret that
such is the case? It is impossible to think so. The
President really comes from the people. He is
their representative, and is more fully sustained
by public opinion than by legislative assemblies.
Nor must we forget that such bodies are, by the
nature of things, more liable than he to be controlled by transitory impressions. The reader who
desires to convince himself of this fact, has only to
glance at the resolutions relative to foreign policy,
adopted by the House of Representatives from time
to time. This body, so remarkable from many
other stand-points, is liable at certain periods to be
carried away in quest of the most unsubstantial
popularity. Then all restraints are disregarded.
Without going further back than 1864, nothing is
hazarded by saying that, if its policy in regard to
Mexico had then prevailed, war would probably
have ensued between France and the United States.
In 1866, with a view of gaining some Irish votes,
it passed a bill which, had it become a law, would
at one blow have destroyed the whole neutrality
policy created by Washington and continued by
all his successors. In 1870 it was scarcely more
prudent on the subject of Cuban affairs. Clearly,

these criticisms do not apply to the Senate. It has almost always evinced a prudent reserve on such questions. But why has this been so? The answer is obvious. This body is more directly in communication with the President; and forming, as will soon be seen, his executive council, it partakes, to a certain degree, the grave responsibility that he incurs. This important distinction should be carefully considered by those who favor the omnipotence of legislative assemblies. Many theorists hold that, representing the people directly, the legislative power is more favorably situated than any other to decide the weightiest matters growing out of the foreign relations of the country, and that the power of making war and peace should be lodged exclusively with it. Nevertheless, the experience of the United States attests that the executive has alone evinced in a very marked degree a sense of responsibility, and although public opinion would have nearly always justified it in exercising an influence over Congress to further an aggressive and menacing policy toward other nations, it has continually restrained, by its prudent moderation, the ill effects that might have resulted from the precipitate action of the House of Representatives.

CHAPTER VI.

RELATIONS OF THE PRESIDENT TO THE JUDICIAL POWER OF THE UNION.

THIS is not the place to investigate the very interesting questions connected with the judicial power, or the organization of the courts of the United States. The constitutional relations existing between them and the President will alone be considered.

Although by the Constitution the three powers are "equal, co-ordinate and independent," nevertheless the judicial branch occupies a peculiar position in regard to Congress and the President. It does not, in the first place, emanate from the people. It consists of judges appointed for life, who, by this very circumstance, are gradually raised above the impure and troubled atmosphere of party passions. Hence its relative weakness as compared with the other powers, and its imposing moral weight upon the more intelligent classes of society.

At the same time the federal courts are in many respects dependent. The Constitution declares: "The judicial power of the United States shall be vested in one Supreme Court, and in such inferior

courts as the Congress may, from time to time,
ordain and establish."[1]

Congress is, without doubt, bound to respect this
constitutional provision; but, in conforming to it,
may still maintain a preponderance over the
judicial department. If it desires, it may, undoubtedly, restrict the appellate jurisdiction of the
Supreme Court. It may also enact, as was proposed in 1868, that this court shall not affirm the
unconstitutionality of an act of Congress, unless
two-thirds of the judges present concur in the decision.[2] It can also increase or diminish the number
of judges, so as to modify, almost at discretion, the
constitution of the court. On the other hand, the
President exercises a considerable influence over the
judicial power. It must not be forgotten, that in
fact he appoints all the federal judges. As
vacancies happen he can, by the selections he
makes to fill them, modify the character of the
court.

Notwithstanding the very peculiar *status* of the Supreme Court, parties on several occasions endeavored
to compel it to play a political part of the highest importance. These various attempts were made under
the following circumstances. At the close of the
presidency of John Adams, the Federal party retired

[1] Constitution, Article III. Sec. 1.

[2] The House Representatives adopted this measure the 13th of
January, 1868. (See McPherson's Political Manual, 1868, pp. 90–91.)

trom power, having lost the control not only of the executive, but also of the two branches of Congress. From the formation of the American Government leading Federalists tried to build up a strong central power. The judicial authority, however, answered but very imperfectly their designs. Hamilton himself said that it was the weakest branch of the government. To use his own words: "The judiciary, on the contrary, has no influence over either the sword or the purse.........and can take no active resolution whatever." He desired to render the executive preponderating power, but in 1800 he had no longer a choice.

In this situation the Federalists decided to give to the judicial power a sort of supreme control. Having so resolved, it was necessary first to strengthen its organization. To this end they agreed to increase the number of courts and also of judges, and at the same time to extend their jurisdiction. The hours of power yet remaining to this party were already numbered when it seized the occasion to pass a bill through Congress which met their wishes, and to secure the approval of Mr. Adams. At the last moment the President sent to the Senate, for its confirmation, the names of forty-two judges. This was done during the day of March 2d, 1801. On the evening of the third these nominations were confirmed, and the morning of the fourth President Jefferson was inaugurated.

He found, on the table of the State Department, the commissions of some of these magistrates, signed by his predecessor, countersigned by the Secretary of State, and attested with the official seal. Jefferson ordered that they should be neither registered nor delivered, but be considered as void. This act furnished the Federalists an opportunity to attack him, and they could rely upon the support of the Supreme Court, with John Marshall at its head. One of the magistrates, Marbury, whose commission had been thus withheld, instituted proceedings in that court against James Madison, then Secretary of State, and applied for a *mandamus*, requiring that officer to deliver it. President Jefferson understood at once the full bearing of this movement. He therefore directed Mr. Madison and all of the employees of the State Department not to enter their appearance to the suit. At the December term, 1801, a motion was made for a rule against Mr. Madison to show cause why a *mandamus* ought not to be issued. Madison failed to plead. The matter was then argued. The following is an analysis of the celebrated decision pronounced on this occasion by Chief Justice Marshall, in which he elaborately discussed the following questions :

1. Has the plaintiff a right to the commission to which he lays claim? 2. If he has such right, and it has been violated, do the laws of the country

furnish him a remedy? 3. If this is admitted to be so, is the remedy to be found in a *mandamus* granted by the Supreme Court? After having answered the first question in the affirmative, the learned judge proceeded : "The very essence of civil liberty certainly consists in the right of every individual to claim the protection of the laws, whenever he receives an injury. One of the first duties of government is to afford that protection. In Great Britain the king himself is sued in the respectful form of a petition, and he never fails to comply with the judgment of his court."

The Chief Justice here cited Blackstone in support of his opinion. According to the English commentator, wherever there is a legal right there is a legal remedy, when that right is invaded or withheld. The opinion then proceeded : "The government of the United States has been emphatically termed a government of laws, and not of men. It will certainly cease to deserve this high appellation if the laws furnish no remedy for the violation of a vested legal right." "Is the act of delivering or witholding a commission to be considered as a mere political act, belonging to the Executive Department alone, for the performance of which entire confidence is placed by our Constitution in the supreme executive, for any misconduct respecting which the injured individual has no remedy ? "

He admitted, then, that without doubt circum-
9

stances might occur in which a recourse to the courts would be impossible; but he refused to declare that every act committed by one of the great branches of the government ought to be classed in this category.

He established on this subject the following distinction: "By the Constitution of the United States the President is invested with certain important political powers, in the exercise of which he is to use his own discretion, and is accountable only to his country in his political character and to his own conscience. To aid him in the performance of these duties he is authorized to apppoint certain officers, who act by his authority and in conformity with his orders." "In such cases their acts are his acts, and whatever opinion may be entertained of the manner in which executive discretion may be used, still there exists, and can exist, no power to control that discretion. The subjects are political. They respect the nation, not individual rights, and being intrusted to the executive, the decision of the executive is conclusive. The application of this remark will be perceived by adverting to the act of Congress for establishing the department of foreign affairs. This officer, as his duties were prescribed by that act, is to conform precisely to the will of the President. He is the mere organ by whom that will is communicated. The acts of such an officer can never be examinable by the courts."

"But when the Legislature proceeds to impose on that officer other duties; when he is directed peremptorily to perform certain acts; when the rights of individuals are dependent on the performance of those acts, he is so far the officer of the law—is amenable to the laws for his conduct, and cannot at his discretion sport away the vested rights of others." The Chief Justice said, in conclusion, that "The question whether a right has vested or not is in its nature judicial, and must be tried by the judicial authority. If, for example, Mr. Marbury has taken the oath of a magistrate, and proceeded to act as one; in consequence of which a suit has been instituted against him, in which his defense depended on his being a magistrate, the validity of his appointment must have been determined by judicial authority."

Such was the Federal doctrine announced by the Chief Justice in this case. But what is remarkable, the judge who had just argued with such forcible logic the question of the relations subsisting between the Judicial and the Executive Powers was constrained to conclude that the Supreme Court, in the exercise of its original jurisdiction, could not award the writ. That jurisdiction was prescribed by the Constitution and could not be enlarged or diminished by act of Congress.

"Still," said he, "to render the *mandamus* a proper remedy, the officer to whom it is to be directed must be one to whom, on legal principles, such writ may be directed, and the person applying for it must be without any other specific and legal remedy. First, with respect to the officer to whom it would be directed. The intimate political relations subsisting between the President of the United States and the heads of departments necessarily renders any legal investigation of the acts of one of those high officers peculiarly irksome, as well as delicate."

Thus, after having several times demonstrated the principles previously enunciated, he concluded by rejecting the claim of Marbury upon jurisdictional grounds alone. So that the judicial power explicitly affirmed the doctrine, that where the law imposes upon an executive officer a *ministerial* act not involving the exercise of judgment or discretion, a mandamus would lie when a proper case arises, but that the courts could not interfere with the President or his subordinates in the discharge of their political duties. This distinction has been recognized and enforced by the Supreme Court in an unbroken series of decisions; and in a leading case under the following circumstances:

The Thirty-ninth Congress, at its last session, (1866-67) passed a first measure—so called—of *reconstruction*, which was subsequently completed, and in many respects made more stringent by the act of 23d March, 1867. Mississippi raised the constitutional question before the Supreme Court, by a bill in chancery, praying that the President of the United States and the general commanding the military district in which this State was comprised, be enjoined from executing these laws. The court dismissed the bill. Chief Justice Chase gave the opinion. Although less emphatic in tone than that of his great predecessor Marshall, in Marbury against Madison, it distinctly declares that the judicial power cannot take cognizance of the political acts of the President. " It is true," said he, " that in the instance before us the interposition of the court is not sought to enforce action by the executive under constitutional legislation, but to restrain such action under legislation alleged to be unconstitutional. But we are unable to perceive that this circumstance takes the case out of the general principle which forbids judicial interference with the exercise of executive discretion. The Congress," continues the opinion, "is the legislative department of the government; the President is the executive department; neither can be restrained in its action by the judicial department, though the acts of both, when performed, are in proper cases subject to its cognizance." And here the opinion makes this important observation. "If the President refuse obedience, it is needless to observe the court is without power to enforce its process. If on the other hand the President complies with the order of the

court, and refuses to execute the act of Congress,
is it not clear that a collision may occur between
the executive and legislative departments of the
government? May not the House of Representatives impeach the President for such refusal?
And in that case could this court interpose in behalf of the President, thus endangered by compli-
ance with its mandate, and restrain by injunction
the Senate of the United States from sitting as a
court of impeachment?"[1] Thus the political action
of the President completely escapes examination
by the courts of justice. It remains to consider in
what way an act of Executive Power falls under
their jurisdiction.

It is almost impossible to give fixed rules in this
respect. No uniform law has attempted to declare
them, and the doctrine of the court has naturally
varied in different cases, so that it is advisable only
to show in what manner the Supreme Court has,
under certain circumstances, asserted and vindi-
cated private rights. One of the most important
causes decided by it is that relating to the legality
of military commissions. During the war of secession those who took the broadest views of
Executive Power maintained that the President
could declare martial law not only in the insurgent districts, but also in the loyal States wherever conspiracies occurred which threatened the

1 Political Manual for 1867, by McPherson, p. 113.

public safety. Indiana was thus placed under this exceptional rule. The executive had ordered the arrest of several individuals, and, what was still more serious, created a military commission for their trial. Among others, one Milligan was tried by it and condemned to death. It is proper to observe, also, that the President's power suspending the privilege of the writ of *habeas corpus* in the loyal States had been approved by Congress. In this situation of affairs Milligan resorted to the district court, and grounded his claim to relief upon the incompetence of the commission to try and condemn a person not in the military service of the United States. The cause was appealed to the Supreme Court. His counsel discussed the questions involved in all their aspects. On the other side, the United States vigorously maintained the order of the President. Finally the court rendered its judgment. The majority of the judges declared the proceedings illegal, and ordered Milligan to be set at liberty. Their opinion sets forth that "the provisions of that instrument on the administration of criminal justice are too plain and direct to leave room for misconstruction or doubt of their true meaning. Those applicable to this case are found in that clause of the original Constitution which says that 'the trial of all crimes, except in case of impeachment, shall be by jury.'

"But it is said that the jurisdiction is complete under the 'laws and usages of war'.........this court has judicial knowledge that in Indiana the federal authority was always unopposed, and its courts always open.........Congress could grant no such power."

What has just been given suffices, without here reproducing the entire argument, to show that the judicial power could effectually interpose to protect the liberty of a citizen against the combined action of the executive and the Legislature. [1]

This judgment was rendered the 17th December, 1866. The civil war then at an end; the order declaring martial law in the loyal States had been revoked. Therefore the Supreme Court could not modify the situation, and it limited itself, if we may say so, to declaring and maintaining the rights guaranteed by the Constitution to the citizen. But suppose that the opinion and judgment had been pronounced during the continuance of the armed struggle. What course would the executive have adopted? Perhaps it would have resolved to disregard them. In such case the Supreme Court could only have repeated the protest of Chief Justice Taney on another occasion: " I have exercised all the power which the Constitution and laws confer on me, but that power has been

[1] Political Manual for 1867, by McPherson, p. 83 *et seq*, and 4 Wallace pp. 121-22.

resisted by a force too strong for me to overcome," and awaited its justification by the public sentiment of the country.[1] But if, on the contrary, the President had obeyed the decision, and liberated Milligan, he would not have been thereby compelled to abolish military commissions in the loyal States. He would simply have said that the decision was only binding in that case, and so then Milligan alone would have been benefited by it. We must not, however, conclude from this instance, occurring as it did during the perils and agitations of a civil war, that in ordinary times the executive fails to manifest an earnest desire to accept and abide by the decisions of the Supreme Court, whenever a case arises to which they apply.

We give one example among a thousand to show the ordinary course of proceedings. The President was authorized by the law of neutrality of 1794 to detain all vessels which had been fitted out and armed within the ports or waters of the United States, for violation of its prohibitions or provisions.[2] The President, in 1816, ordered the collector of the port of New-York to seize and detain a suspected vessel. The detention was continued by him for some time without taking the required steps to bring her before the proper court for adju-

1 Law Reporter, June, 1861, p. 89 exparte Merryman.

2 This provision again appears in the act commonly known as the neutrality act, adopted in 1818, and now in force.

dication. The proprietors then resorted to judicial proceedings to determine whether the prerogative of the President implied a right unduly to prolong the duration of an arbitrary seizure. On appeal to the Supreme Court it was held that the President could not detain a vessel, except during the time necessary to carry the case before the courts.[1]

Since then the Executive Power has made no difficulty in conforming its action in such cases to this decision.

Thus, in 1869, when Spain was building thirty gunboats in New York, Peru, alleging that there still existed a state of war between her and Spain, requested the President of the United States to detain them provisionally. Although no proof was furnished of the truth of the allegation, he consented to exercise the power granted him by the neutrality act, and in consequence forbade the launching of them; but as Perú took no further step in the matter, he, in view of the decision of the Supreme Court, soon directed their release. In recapitulating what has been said upon the relations of the executive to the Supreme Court, it is well to notice:

1. That the judicial authority must avoid interfering with the legislative and political functions of the President. It can neither constrain him to execute or to oppose a law.

[1] Slocum vs. Mayberry et al., 2 Wheaton p. 1 *et seq.*

2. That in the greater number of cases the Judicial Power, when it has jurisdiction of a cause, protects the constitutional or vested rights of a citizen against the encroachments of the Executive or the Legislative Power. Its decisions, as a general thing, constitute a jurisprudence full of wisdom. They are consulted by the other branches of the government, and considered of the highest authority.

But we cannot close this chapter without specially adverting to the right which the Supreme Court has almost constantly asserted of deciding, as a tribunal of last resort, upon the constitutionality of laws. In fact it has not simply limited its action to the interpretation of the laws and the establishment of its jurisprudence; but at certain epochs has assumed to impose its opinions upon other branches of the federal government, and render judgments upon the validity of their acts. In the decision in Marbury against Madison, Chief Justice Marshall clearly asserted this claim. He says "That the people have an original right to establish, for their future government, such principles as in their opinion shall most conduce to their own happiness; it is the base on which the whole American fabric has been erected. The exercise of this original right is a very great exertion; nor can it, nor ought it, to be frequently repeated. The principles, therefore, so established, are deemed fundamental, and as the authority from which they proceed is supreme, and can seldom act, they are designed to be permanent. This original and supreme will organizes the government, and assigns to different departments their respective powers. It may either stop here, or establish certain limits not to be transcended by those departments." The opinion then establishes that the powers of the Legislature are defined and limited, by a written Constitution, in order that Congress should not exceed them. If then a legislative act be contrary to the Constitution, it follows as an inevitable conclusion, inasmuch as that instrument is of paramount authority, that such act "is not law."

The Chief Justice deduced from these principles the following conclusion: If an act of the Legislature is void, it cannot bind the courts, and they are not, therefore, obliged to put it in execution. "It is emphatically the province and duty of the judicial department to say what the law is. Those who apply the rule to particular cases must of necessity expound and interpret that rule. If two laws conflict with each other, the courts must decide on the operation of each. So if a law be in opposition to the Constitution, if both the law and the Constitution apply to a particular case, so that the court must either decide that case conformably to the law, disregarding the Constitution, or conformably to the Constitution, disregarding the law, the court must determine which of these conflicting rules govern the case. This is of the very essence of judicial duty.[1]

Moreover, the text of the Constitution of the United States confirms this opinion : " The judicial power shall extend to all cases arising under this Constitution." What meaning could be given to this clause, if the tribunals had not the right of interpretation ?

The principles deduced with so much force by Chief Justice Marshall, are incontestably sound, as applied to the judicial power. No one has doubted the power of the courts to determine the constitutionality of a law, when the question arises, in any pending suit, within their jurisdiction. But the point now under discussion is, whether their decision upon constitutional questions establishes a rule which binds the other branches of the government. In a word, is the Legislature or the executive compelled to consider as unconstitutional an act declared to be such by the Supreme Court, or as one of the disciples of John Marshall said, does the power of interpreting the laws necessarily imply that of examining, if they are in accordance with the Constitution, and is the judgment of that court, declaring them null and void, conclusive ?[2]

[1] Cranch's Reports, pp. 131 *et seq.*
[2] Commentaries on the Constitution of the United States by Mr. Justice Story, ¶ 1570.

Such is the question in all its breadth. If Marshall did not present it in its full extent, Story went further. Moreover, we must observe that this eminent magistrate and commentator wrote at the moment when the discussion relative to the right of interpretation claimed by the Supreme Court was about to be renewed.

In fact, the old Republican party of Jefferson, which had become, under President Jackson, the Democratic party, had never for a moment ceased to protest against the constitutional prerogatives that the judicial power assumed to maintain. Under these circumstances the question again came up on the subject of the United States Bank.

Although the Supreme Court had declared that the act incorporating the bank was constitutional, yet President Jackson, as mentioned in one of the preceding chapters, vetoed the act renewing its charter. It was insisted by the advocates of the bank that its constitutionality, in all its features, ought to be considered as settled by precedent and by the decision of the Supreme Court. But he protested against that doctrine, and observed that "without the consent of the people the Supreme Court could not decide questions of this class. The Congress, the Executive and the Court must each for itself be guided by its own opinion of the Constitution. Each public officer who takes an oath to support the Constitution swears that he will support it as he understands it, and not as it is understood by others. The opinion of the judges has no more authority over Congress than the opinion of Congress has over the judges, and on that point the President is independent of both. The authority of the Supreme Court must not, therefore, be permitted to control the Congress or the executive when acting in their legislative capacities."[1]

The Whig party adhered to the Federal doctrine, and Mr. Webster defended it with all the force of his talent, yet the prevailing words of this discussion, so far as we can judge at present, were uttered by a Democratic Senator from Tennessee, who was assuredly not the intellectual equal of the great Whig orator.

"The honorable Senator," said Mr. White, "argues that the Constitution has constituted the Supreme Court a tribunal to decide great constitutional questions such as this, and that when they have done so, the question is put at rest, and every other department of the government must acquiesce. This doctrine I deny. The Constitution vests 'the judicial power in a Supreme Court, and in such inferior courts as Congress may from time to time ordain and establish.' Whenever a suit is commenced and prosecuted in the courts of the United States, of which they have jurisdiction, and

[1] Thirty Years' View, Vol. I., p. 252.

suit is decided by the Supreme Court—as that is
the court of last resort—its decision is final and
conclusive between the parties. But as an authority it does not bind either the Congress or the
President of the United States.........If different
interpretations are put upon the Constitution by
the different departments, the people is the tribunal to settle the dispute. Each of the departments
is the agent of the people, doing their business according to the powers conferred, and where there
is a disagreement as to the extent of these powers,
the people themselves, through the ballot-boxes,
must settle it."[1]

Such was the opinion of General Jackson and his
leading adherents, in which a majority of the people
acquiesced.

Twenty-five years later the Democratic party
repudiated these doctrines. Relying upon the sympathies of a majority of the Supreme Court, they
asserted the binding authority of judicial interpretation. On the other hand, the new Republican
party, although rather allied by its principles to
the old Federal school, espoused the doctrine of
President Jackson. Thus, by a strange turning
over, the Democrats in 1857 became the disciples
of Hamilton, and the Republicans, of Jefferson.

At that date the question of the power of Con-

1 Political Parties in the United States, by Martin Van Buren,
p. 311 *et seq.*

gress over slavery in the territories was profoundly agitating the Union, and the celebrated case of Dred Scott against Sanford was carried before the Supreme Court. It involved matters which might lead the judges to render a decision bearing upon the political issues of the day. The court might have given its opinion during the term of 1855–56, but as the presidential election was impending, the judges thought it best to postpone the judgment.

President Buchanan was inaugurated March 4th, 1857. In his address on that occasion he said that a difference of opinion had arisen as to the time when the inhabitants of a territory were authorized to decide for themselves the question of slavery. "Besides," added he, "it is a judicial question which legitimately belongs to the Supreme Court of the United States, before whom it is now pending, and will, it is understood, be speedily and finally settled. To their decision, in common with all good·citizens, I shall cheerfully submit."[1]

Two days later the decision was pronounced. Its doctrines need not be here analyzed. It is sufficient to say, that never had the Federalists pushed further the legislative assumptions of the Supreme. Court.[2]

1 Inaugural address of President James Buchanan.

2 The American Conflict, by Horace Greeley, p. 251. Mr. Buchanan's Administration, p. 50.

Nevertheless this decision was not received as final. The President asked in vain, that it should be so considered. The Republicans replied, as General Jackson had formerly done, that, although conclusive upon Dred Scott and Sanford, the parties to the suit wherein it was rendered, it had no binding effect upon the country. They protested vehemently against the doctrines it announced. Then, as Mr. Buchanan himself observes in a published defense of his administration, the agitation continued for years, just as if the Supreme Court had not spoken.

And March 4th, 1861, President Lincoln mentions the subject in the following manner: "Constitutional questions are to be decided by the Supreme Court; nor do I deny that such decision must be binding in any case upon the parties to a suit, as to the object of that suit, while they are also entitled to very high respect and consideration in all parallel cases by all other departments of the government.........At the same time the candid citizen must confess that if the policy of the government upon vital questions, affecting the whole people, is to be irrevocably fixed by decisions of the Supreme Court, the instant they are made in ordinary litigation between parties in personal actions, the people will have ceased to be their own rulers, having to that extent practically resigned their government into the hands of that eminent tribunal." [1]

Thus the doctrine of the finality of the decisions of the Supreme Court on constitutional questions has never met with universal acceptance. Sustained by one party, they have been resisted by the other. Under Jefferson and Jackson the executive refused to yield to them; under Buchanan it taught that unhesitating submission to them was the first duty of all good citizens. The Republican party refused to accept as a rule of political action the opinions of that court which asserted the unconstitutionality of federal legislation excluding slavery from the territories. Indeed it could scarcely have been otherwise.

To recapitulate, the three powers are co-ordinate and independent. Each, in the discharge of its appropriate duties, is to decide for itself the constitutionality of laws. Congress determines this question. So does the President, whenever bills are presented for his signature. So must the Supreme Court, in cases within its original or appellate jurisdiction. The judgment of the latter upon the inquiry whether a given law is in accordance with the Constitution is undoubtedly final, so far as the parties to the record are concerned; but the other branches of the government are not bound

[1] Mr. Lincoln's Inaugural Address, March 4th, 1861. McPherson's History of the Rebellion, p. 107.

by it or by the doctrines advanced in the reasoned opinion of the court. So the action of the judicial tribunals is thus necessarily confined within fitting and salutary limits. Charged with the protection of individual rights, they are invested with an authority, the importance of which can be scarcely exaggerated.

It is their duty, in disposing of suits, not only to interpret the enactments which are applicable to the subject-matter in controversy, but to decide whether they are in conflict with the Constitution, and if so, to give to the latter supreme authority. That instrument guarantees almost all the individual rights of the citizen, and when they are assailed by the tyrannical acts of either legislative or Executive Power, the Supreme Court can almost always stretch forth its protecting arm in his defense.

CHAPTER VII.

THE FEDERAL ADMINISTRATION.

THE President is elected in the beginning of November.. The 4th of March following, at noon precisely, the powers of his predecessor expire, and the newly-elected President appears before the people, assembled at the Capitol, and the Chief Justice of the United States administers the constitutional oath. This scene is always impressive, and, under certain circumstances, inspires the nation with the deepest interest.

On the occasion of this solemn ceremony the President makes known to the people his political programme. He has had nearly four months to prepare it and to think over the pledges given by his party during the electoral campaign. He has also, as a general thing, counseled with experienced men. He has not, then, wanted opportunities of informing himself upon the great issues of which he is about to assume the direction, so that his address, at the moment of entering upon office, ought to give the result of his preliminary reflections.

When the President has been re-elected, his situation is infinitely better. He has the advantage of experience; but, even in this event, a new period begins for him at his second inauguration. American politics change every four years, and this is almost as much the case when the President is re-elected as when a new personage makes his appearance.

The address delivered, the chief magistrate takes the following oath: "I do solemnly swear [or affirm] that I will faithfully execute the office of President of the United States, and will, to the best of my ability, preserve, protect and defend the Constitution of the United States." It is thus that he enters on the execution of his office. If, in order to prepare himself for the proper fulfillment of the duties imposed upon him, he limited himself to a study of the text of the Constitution, he would fail to have an exact idea of them. He would there find that he is vested with the power of a suspensive veto, and that it is his duty to take care that the laws be faithfully executed. He would also learn that he is the commander-in-chief of the army and navy of the United States, and of the militia of the several States when called into the actual service of the United States; that he may require the opinion, in writing, of the principal officer in each of the executive departments upon any subject relating to the duties of their respective offices; that he has the power to grant reprieves and pardons for offenses against the United States in cases of impeachment; that he has the power, by and with the advice and consent of the Senate, to make treaties, provided two-thirds of the Senators present concur, and to nominate, and by and with the advice and consent of the Senate, appoint ambassadors, other public ministers and consuls, judges of the Supreme Court, and all other officers of the United States whose appointments are not therein otherwise provided for, and which have been, or shall be, established by law; that he has power to fill up all vacancies that may happen during the recess of the Senate, by granting com- missions which shall expire at the end of their next session; that he shall from time to time give to the Congress information of the state of the Union, and recommend to their consideration such measures as he shall judge necessary and expedient; that he may, on extraordinary occasions, convene both Houses, or either of them, and in case of disa- greement between them, with respect to the time of adjournment, may adjourn them to such time as he shall think proper; that he shall receive ambassadors and other public ministers; and, finally, that he shall commission all the officers of the United State.[1]

Such are his powers and duties, as set forth in

1 Constitution, Article II., Sections 2, 3.

the Constitution.   As may be seen they are quite
undefined. A commentator remarks: "In many respects the most defective part of the Federal Constitution, beyond all question, is that which relates
to the executive departments.   It is impossible to
read that instrument without being forcibly struck
with the loose and unguarded terms in which
the powers and duties of the President are pointed
out.........but in regard to the executive the convention appears to have studiously selected such
loose and general expressions as would enable the
President, by implication and construction, either
to neglect his duties or to enlarge his powers." [1]

But, on the other hand, it is almost certain that,
if the convention had been more definite, the Constitution could not have withstood the trials to
which it has been exposed. That it has done so is
owing to the fact that there is in reality in the
United States an Executive Power for time of
peace, and another adapted to times of commotion
or war. Then, so far from concurring in the opinion of the commentator, those who study American
institutions will be lead to conclude that the article
of the Constitution which is the subject of his
criticism is one of the most skillfully conceived, by
reason of the very general and somewhat indefinite
phraseology used by its framers.

1 Upshur on Nature and Character of our Federal Government.
Ed. 1863, pp. 116–119.

Indeed, the organization of the Executive Power in a republican form of government always presents the greatest difficulties. If its powers are defined with exact precision, events may at some critical juncture occur which will baffle all calculations. Then the republic will be placed between the danger of violating its fundamental law and the imperious necessities of public safety. Now it is much to be feared that, in moments of imminent peril, the majority would decide in favor of usurpations of power, and suffer the Constitution to be sacrificed. The only means of avoiding these dangers is to mould the fundamental law so that the President, always prominent in times of crisis, may be able to stretch his privileges, in case circumstances shall absolutely require it.

It is needless to dwell upon this point; political history shows its full importance. Why have so many written constitutions, monarchical or republican, proved utter failures? It is because they have almost always been constructed so logically that their framers attempted to provide for all the contingencies of an unknown future. They thus exhausted the resources of their genius in an impracticable programme; but the work so laboriously constructed was overthrown by the first political convulsion that occurred. Happily for the United States, the framers of the Constitution pursued an entirely different course; they vested certain powers in the President, but did not declare that these powers should form a limit to his authority. Besides, the prerogatives thus conferred upon him admit on certain occasions of an almost indefinite extension.

In examining the constitutional provisions relative to the President, it is first of all to be noticed that he has certain powers which belong properly to him alone. Others, on the contrary, are exercised under the supervision of a great council of the government which the Constitution has associated with him. If he shall take care that the laws be faithfully executed, command the army and navy of the United States, receive ambassadors and other public ministers, and grant reprieves and pardons for offenses against the United States without being subject to any restraint, he is not allowed to conclude treaties, nor appoint the principal public functionaries, without the concurrent action of the Senate. In such matters, that high assembly no longer forms a part of the legislative power, but is transformed, so to express it, into a sort of family council, whose advice the President is required to take.

It is fitting, then, first to examine into those powers conferred solely on the President, and afterward allude to those which he cannot execute without the intervention of the Senate.

Pursuant to the constitutional provisions above

mentioned, Congress organized, at the formation of the Government, the principal executive departments which were to be placed under the immediate direction of the President.

An act of July 27th, 1789, created the State Department, and confided to it the conduct of foreign affairs. Another act, of September 15th of the same year, conferred upon it certain other powers of a different nature, and among them that of promulgating the laws. Its jurisdiction has been still further extended by subsequent legislation.

The organization of the Treasury Department dates September 2d, 1789. The act of Congress creating it defined the extent of its powers, and charged it with the management of the federal finances.

The War Department was established the 7th of August of the same year. Since then its powers have been modified, augmented or diminished, according to the necessities of the hour.

The Navy Department was organized April 21st, 1806.

The general post-office was formed into a separate department March 3d, 1825.

Finally, the Department of the Interior was constituted by the act of March 3d, 1849.

Thus, the navy, the postal service and the branches of the service under the supervision of the Department of the Interior were successively detached from the State, Treasury, and War Departments.

But this is not all. At the formation of the government Congress provided for the appointment of a functionary, whose special duty it is to interpret the laws, act as the legal adviser of the President and heads of departments, and represent the United States before the Supreme Court. Such is the province of the Attorney-general, as declared by an act of September 4, 1789. He is at the same time a member of the Cabinet, and a sort of solicitor-general before the Supreme Court, and was destined, in the legislative thought, to play a part of the highest importance near the executive. Experience has since proved that the Attorney-general is in reality one of the most considerable functionaries of the government. [1]

Thus the creation of these several departments places under the immediate direction of the Executive Power foreign affairs, finances, the army, the navy, the post-offices, the branches of the service relative to the management, sale and disposal of the public lands, to pensions, to patents for inventions in the useful arts, and to Indian affairs. It likewise secures a legal adviser to the President and a representative of the entire government before the Supreme Court. In a word, Congress, in organizing the public administration, confided to the Executive Power the duty of directing it. In

[1] Brightly's Digest. See the table of contents and the laws which are therein cited.

order to see how it has been fulfilled it is necessary
to pass in review the foreign policy, the organization of the army and navy, the financial system of
the government and its jurisprudence as established
by the Attorney-general.

FOREIGN AFFAIRS.

As Pinckney said in the convention of 1787,
those who devote themselves to the great work of
forming the American republic must renounce, in
the conduct of foreign affairs, the traditions of
European policy. So the relations of the new
republic with foreign powers should be as slight as
the essential interests of the country would allow.
Such was the principle that Washington was soon
to apply. Events soon forced him to determine
what should be the foreign policy of the United
States. At the time when the Federal Government went into operation the states general were
on the point of meeting at Versailles, so that almost
at the same date when the national life of the United
States commenced, France was preparing those
changes which were so seriously to affect the institutions of the old world. As the French revolution progressed, it attracted more and more
deeply the attention of the United States. Had
not the co-operation of France been of incalcu-
lable advantage to the thirteen colonies? Was
there not apparently a perfect similarity between

the principles proclaimed on the American continent in 1776, and those imposed by the Constituent
Assembly on French royalty?

In fact, the sympathies of a great number of
Americans were enlisted in the movements of which
France was the theater.   But in 1793 the position
of the United States had changed.   They were to
consider if the war which had just broken out between the French convention and England would
not be likely to constrain them to take an active
part in these hostilities. On the one side was France,
who had given the aid of her sword to the cause
of American independence; on the other, England,
against whom the thirteen colonies had sustained
a long struggle.   What was Washington to do?
Under these decisive circumstances he announced,
for the first time in the world, the principle that
"every nation has a right to remain neutral whilst
other nations are at war."

"The critical and irritable state of things in
France," says his biographer, "began so materially
to affect the United States as to require an exertion of all the prudence and all the firmness of the
government.   The 10th of August, 1792, was succeeded in that nation by such a state of anarchy and
by scenes of so much blood and horror; the nation
was understood to be so divided with respect to its
future course, and the republican party was threatened by such formidable external force, that there

was much reason to doubt whether the fallen monarch would be finally deposed, or reinstated with a greater degree of splendor and power than the constitution just laid in ruins had assigned to him."

Gouverneur Morris then represented the United States in France. President Washington, sending him instructions, said "the American administration entertained no doubt of the propriety of recognizing the existing authority of France, whatever form it might assume; that every nation possessed a right to govern. itself according to its own will, to change its institutions at discretion, and to transact its business through whatever agents it might think proper........."

"Such are the principles upon which the American government is itself established, and it cannot deny to another nation the right to apply them." Beside, the United States Minister was to assure the French people that America entertained for them the sincerest sympathy.

"Yet," he adds, "that, devoted to the principles of real liberty, and approving unequivocally the republican form of government, he hoped for a favorable result from the efforts which were making to establish that form by the great ally of the United States, but was not so transported by those efforts as to involve his country in their issue." Washington also observed that the aid to American independence had been given by the old royalty.

It was then the fixed purpose of the President to maintain the neutrality of the United States, however general the war might be in Europe. In the meantime, in the beginning of April, 1793, the federal government was apprised of the declaration of war by France against England and Holland. This event awakened all the ardor of feeling that ten years of peace had not extinguished. The prejudices against England, which had become so deep-seated during the revolutionary war, seemed again to revive. A great portion of the American people considered it criminal for the United States to remain indifferent spectators of a conflict between their former enemy and the French Republic.

"The feeling upon this occasion was almost universal.........the war was confidently and generally pronounced a war of aggression on the part of Great Britain, undertaken for the sole purpose of imposing a monarchical government on the French people...... Yet the disposition to engage in the war was far from being general." [1]

It was for President Washington to decide what should be the foreign policy of the republic. Was he to be led away by the popular current? Could he, on the contrary, resist it? A statesman, who bears with honor the greatest historic name of the United States, Mr. Charles Francis Adams, describes in the following manner what then took place:

[1] The Life of George Washington, by John Marshall, Vol. V., p. 398 *et seq.*

" To that council Washington had carefully elected two of the ablest and best qualified statesmen
that the great struggle for liberty had produced, the
only drawback to which was the misfortune that
they scarcely ever could agree; the one, abounding
in capacity, leaned to speculation and theory, to
which he sought to accommodate facts; the other,
equally gifted, preferred to view the facts first, and
from them form his theories afterward. The first
had a synthetic, the other an analytic, mind........Yet
between these discordant elements it was the pecu.
liar faculty of Washington to be able to educe from
each most valuable contributions to the regulation
of his policy. They never served him better than
in the present emergency. The sixteen questions
were submitted on the 18th of April, 1793. On the
next day all four of the Cabinet had united in an
affirmative answer to the first, which was the essential one."

It ran in the following words: "Shall a proclamation issue for the purpose of preventing inter-
ferences of the citizens of the United States in the
war between France and Great Britain ?" Another
question—whether the minister, known to be on
his way as a representative from the new republic,
should be received, was also unanimously agreed
to. And here the President was fain to stop; for
the opposing forces, Jefferson and Hamilton, fell
into such differences upon the remaining questions

11

that it was weeks before they got through their expositions. This was of no consequence, as from the one answer he laid the great foundation of his policy. A proclamation was immediately drawn up and issued on the 22d of April, 1793. The substantial part was in these words :

" WHEREAS, it appears that a state of war exists between Austria, Prussia, Sardinia, Great Britain and the United Netherlands on the one part, and France on the other ; and the duty and interest of the United States require that they should, with sincerity and good faith, adopt and pursue *a conduct friendly and impartial toward the belligerent powers.*" Washington then gave notice of the neutrality of the United States; and he warned "the citizens of the United States carefully to avoid all acts and proceedings whatsoever which may in any manner tend to contravene such disposition." [1]

At the opening of the following session of Congress, the 2d December of the same year, the President announced to Congress the policy that he had adopted. At the very time when he had just published this proclamation of April 22d, containing almost all the foreign policy of the United States, the minister of the French republic arrived at Charleston.

Edmund Genet, brother of Madam Campan, had

1 Address of Hon. Charles Francis Adams, delivered before the New York Historical Society, Dec. 13th, 1870.

received some diplomatic training under the old *régime;* his last post had been that of *Charge d'affaires* to Russia. The revolutionary attitude which he then assumed had brought him to the notice of the dominant party in Paris. As his instructions directed him to neglect nothing to force the United States to take part in the war, he thought it good policy to land first at Charleston. He supposed that in this city, remote from the seat of government, he could readily render himself master of the situation. He at once commenced distributing commissions and arming privateers.

During the nine months that his mission lasted, Genet either tried to elude the neutrality policy of the government, or opposed it directly. Everywhere he labored to arouse popular prejudices against the administration, and everywhere he was met by its unflinching determination. It is to be regretted that no one has ever taken the pains to write a circumstantial account of the diplomacy of this French *sans-culotte;* his pompous declarations, his revolutionary verbosity ought to be contrasted with the calm resolution and dignified language of the rulers of the American republic. But however much he may have succeeded in exciting the vulgar passions of the masses, he could not triumph over the President or his Cabinet. At the end of several months Washington peremptorily-demanded and obtained his recall.

The neutrality of the United States had thus been maintained in their relations with France. It was now to be jeopardized by England. This latter nation had for the preceding ten years maintained an attitude of sullen indifference. When the armed struggle commenced between her and France, an order in council struck a cruel blow at the commerce of the United States. At the same time hostile indications were manifested in Canada. Congress became in turn excited, and retaliatory measures were proposed; the times were critical.

Washington watched the progress of events with anxious attention. He determined to make a last effort in favor of his policy of neutrality. With this view he created a special mission to England, and confided it to John Jay, Chief Justice of the United States. A treaty was soon concluded, and hostilities thus avoided. It was no sooner signed, however, than it became the subject of violent opposition. The press abounded in assaults upon it, and popular assemblies denounced it in their resolutions. Washington, on one occasion, made the following reply:

"Without a predilection for my own judgment, I have weighed with attention every argument which has at any time been brought into view. But the Constitution is the guide which I never can abandon. It has assigned to the President the power of making treaties with the advice and con-

sent of the Senate. It was doubtless supposed that
these two branches of government would combine,
without passion and with the best means of information, those facts and principles upon which the
success of our foreign relations will always depend ;
that they ought not to substitute for their own con
viction the opinions of others, or to seek truth
through any channel but that of a temperate and
well informed investigation. Under this persua-
sion I have resolved on the manner of executing
the duty before me; to the high responsibility
attached to it I freely submit."[1]

Thus did Washington inaugurate the neutrality
of the United States; he had maintained it with
regard to France and afterward caused it to be
accepted by England. But his task was not yet
completed. The effect produced in France by the
treaty concluded between the United States and
England was, as might have been expected,
extremely unfavorable. The directory manifested,
as the convention had done, the utmost resentment.
At that moment General Bonaparte triumphed in
Italy; the French government then thought itself
in a condition to make unreasonable demands upon
the United States. It was also fully aware that the
foreign policy of Washington was violently attacked
by portions of the American people.

In the meantime Washington retired from pub-

1 Washington's Writings, edited by Sparks, Vol. I., p. 505.

lic life, bequeathing to his country his foreign policy. It is fully explained in a memorable paper, the farewell address of that great man.

"In the execution of such a plan," said he, "nothing is more essential than that permanent, inveterate antipathies against particular nations, and passionate attachments for others, should be excluded, and that, in place of them, just and amicable feelings toward all should be cultivated. The nation which indulges toward another an habitual hatred, or an habitual fondness, is in some degree a slave. It is a slave to its animosity or to its affection, either of which is sufficient to lead it astray from its duty and its interest. Antipathy in one nation against another disposes each more readily to offer insult and injury, to lay hold of slight causes of umbrage, and to be haughty and intractable when accidental or trifling occasions of dispute occur. Hence frequent collisions, obstinate, envenomed and bloody contests. The nation, prompted by ill will and resentment, sometimes impels to war the government, contrary to the best calculations of policy. The government sometimes participates in the national propensity, and adopts, through passion, what reason would reject........."

"So, likewise, a passionate attachment of one nation to another produces a variety of evils. Sympathy for the favorite nation, facilitating the illusion of an imaginary common interest, in cases where no real common interest exists, and infusing into one the enmities of the other, betrays the former into a participation in the quarrels and wars of the latter, without adequate inducement or justi·fication. It leads also to concessions to the favorite nation of privileges denied to others, which is apt doubly to injure the nation making the concessions, by unnecessarily parting with what ought to have been retained, and by exciting jealousy, ill will and a disposition to retaliate, in the parties from whom equal privileges are withheld; and it gives to ambitious, corrupted, or deluded citizens (who devote themselves to the favorite nation), facility to betray or sacrifice the interests of their own country without odium, sometimes even with popularity........."

" Against the insidious wiles of foreign influence (I conjure you to believe me, fellow citizens,) the jealousy of a free people ought to be *constantly* awake; since history and experience prove that foreign influence is one of the most baneful foes of republican government........." "The great rule of conduct for us, in regard to foreign nations, is in extending our commercial relations, to have with them as little *political* connection as · possible. So far as we have already formed engagements, let them be fulfilled with perfect good faith......... Here let us stop."

"Europe has a set of primary interests which to us have no, or a very remote, relation. Hence, she must be engaged in frequent controversies, the causes of which are essentially foreign to our concerns. Hence, therefore, it must be unwise in us to implicate ourselves, by artificial ties, in the ordinary vicissitudes of her politics, or the ordinary combinations and collisions of her friendships or enmities."

" Our detached and distant situation invites and enables us to pursue a different course. If we remain one people, under an efficient government, the period is not far off when we may defy material injury from external annoyance; when we may take such an attitude as will cause the neutrality we may at any time resolve upon to be scrupulously respected; when belligerent nations, under the impossibility of making acquisitions upon us, will not lightly hazard the giving us provocation; when we may choose peace or war, as our interest, guided by justice, shall counsel."

" Why forego the advantages of so peculiar a situation? Why quit our own to stand upon foreign ground? Why be interweaving our destiny with that of any part of Europe?........ " " It is our true policy to steer clear of permanent alliances with any portion of the foreign world........."

Washington thus explained in this immortal " address " the policy which he had created and which the United States still upholds. Since his day the most celebrated American state papers on foreign affairs have been but commentaries on this text. Successive parties have held power, and, although differing widely on the domestic policy of the country, have all concurred in regard to its foreign policy. In the midst of the quadrennial changes of the executive, a uniform line of conduct has been maintained at the State Department. The statesmen who have been at its head, from Jefferson down to the present moment, have found, on entering it, the memories of their predecessors, and to this tradition, thus transmitted intact for nearly a century, the federal government is indebted for its almost unvarying diplomatic success.

It is not here proposed to narrate a history so full of interest and instruction. It is sufficient to remark that the application of the doctrines inculcated by Washington enabled Adams and Jefferson to adjust the irritating questions then pending between the United States and France. These last acts completed the system of American neutrality, and led to its acceptance by Europe.

Since then, how many events have taken place! What serious conflicts have burst forth! But despite these violent excitements, the United States have never deviated from this settled policy, and it is proper to add, that by their patience and moderation they have almost always accomplished their objects. The executive is specially entitled to the honor of initiating and adhering to it, and in this Washington and his successors have been the true representatives of the people. It was so clearly foreshadowed in the debates of the Convention of 1787,. that he who runs may read, and Washington, who presided over that body, may have derived from them his first conceptions on the subject. But if the direction of foreign affairs had been confided to Congress, it is almost certain that the United States would have been drawn into European complications. The most distinctive portion, perhaps, of their policy would soon have disappeared, and their condition have become almost similar to that of other nations. Could they then have at once dispensed with a large standing army, and a very great increase of their navy? Gradually military spirit, giving birth in its turn to a passion for conquest, would have been fostered, and American liberty might have perished in the shock of arms.

The policy of neutrality, which appeared to the framers of the Constitution as an inevitable consequence. of republican institutions, is probably destined sooner or later to a general acceptance in the world.

The geographical position of the United States has doubtless singularly favored the independence of their foreign relations, but this cause alone would not suffice for an explanation. Current events in England show that in proportion as countries become more democratic, and through a progressive movement approach more closely to republican institutions, they lose almost insensibly a taste for the policy of diplomacy. The studied combinations, the treaties of alliance secretly prepared, the great schemes of men of genius, who, like Richelieu, had so admirably re-adjusted Europe, wars of equilibrium and of conquest are all of a nature essentially aristocratic. With the removal of the last traces of germanic feudal institutions, will also disappear all that has fostered the grandeur of the societies in which they existed. It remains to be seen how this transformation, which the American democracy was the first fully to accept, and which England, owing to her insular position, regards with increasing favor, can be effected on the continent of Europe. Will the democratic spirit destroy those almost feudal societies, which still cling to the traditions of the past, or will it, on the contrary, be conquered and suppressed? But the solution of this knotty problem will not be attempted here. By the side of old Europe new democratic communities are in process of formation at different points of the globe, thanks to the indo-germanic emigration which is spreading over the whole world.

. Sir Charles Dilke, who has recently visited them, has given a most interesting account of his voyages in "The Greater Britain." In the same category with the United States he places New Zealand and

Australia, societies which are developing with prodigious rapidity, and where a new spirit is breathing in full liberty. In all probability these people of yesterday are destined to perform one day a leading part in the world; and among them will naturally prevail the doctrines of neutrality which sprung from the American democracy, and received their shape from Washington.

It would not certainly be accurate to say that the executive, left to itself, would not have made frequent mistakes in conducting foreign affairs; that despite the teachings of its cherished tradition it would not have yielded at times to fatal influences; but the framers of the Constitution, whilst wisely leaving to that branch of the government the initiative, placed its action under the supervisory control of the Senate. It is only by and with the consent of that body that the President can contract international engagements; a judicious arrangement, to which special reference will hereafter be made. The foreign policy of the United States has relieved them from the necessity of keeping up a large standing army. The system adopted in that regard has been uniformly maintained. It may be applied as well to sea as to land forces, and has essentially affected the financial policy of the government.

THE ARMY AND NAVY.

The convention of 1787 was not in favor of

maintaining standing armies. It deemed a military spirit to be incompatible with a republican form of government. The United States was, however, then surrounded by European colonies; it had also to face the difficulties that the Indians would not fail to stir up. It was therefore necessary to organize a sufficient force. The great maritime and commercial interests of a growing country also required protection, and created the necessity for a navy. "America united," said Mr. Madison, "with a handful of troops, or without a single soldier, exhibits a more forbidding posture to foreign ambition than America disunited, with a hundred thousand veterans ready for combat." But although believing that the Union, cemented and secured by the Constitution, obviated the necessity of large standing armies, and that liberty would be crushed between them and perpetual taxes, he admitted the propriety of organizing and maintaining such land and sea forces as were indispensable. He thought that they would work no danger to free institutions, and declared that suspicion herself ought to blush, in pretending that the representatives of the United States, elected *freely* by the *whole body* of the people, every *second year*, could not be safely intrusted with a discretion over the appropriations for "raising and supporting armies," expressly limited to the short period of *two years !* [1]

1 The "Federalist," p. 278 *et seq.*

In this he was evidently mistaken. Parliaments voting annually contingents, and determining the budget for the army and navy, have in other countries been expelled by military conspiracies from the halls where they deliberated. Thus the American legislator has felt that the precautions taken by the Constitution were not sufficient, and he has therefore added others vastly more efficacious.[1] The army has been limited to a very small number of regiments, stationed at detached posts over the whole United States, and more especially distributed in the immense deserts of the west. In reality, when the country is at peace, the presence of the army is not felt; the citizen rarely meets or comes in contact with a soldier. The eminent officers, who generally command special corps, do not in a greater degree arrest public attention; almost always as capable as modest, they cherish the military spirit and traditions, and keep themselves aloof from political associations. They form a very small circle, and rarely aspire to go beyond it.

Besides, the standing army is deprived of the right of suffrage. Thus, so far from desiring to make use of it, demagogues are at a loss for epithets strong enough to express their dislike for it. This state of things places it in a very peculiar position. It almost feels that it ought not to make itself conspicuous, and that its very existence depends on its extreme reserve. It is also well to notice that, although the President is commander-in-chief, yet he cannot make an instrument of the army. The regulations, which may be called organic, of the War Department, determine the different posts that the army is to occupy. He has doubtless a right to transfer a regiment, but he could not order it to Washington without at once exciting an opposition which he could scarcely resist. In a word, public liberty cannot be threatened by an army so organized that its approach to the capital is impossible.

In reality, the defensive force of the United States does not depend on the regular army. In moments of crisis the entire people are called to arms. The Union contains within its broad territories a population admirably adapted to war. The man best fitted for military service is incontestably he who unites to a high measure of intelligence and of education that habit of self-dependence which is gradually lost in those communities where the principle of a division of labor has been fully developed. The settler in the forest or the plains, whose arm has felled the trees, built his cabin and guided his plowshare through the virgin soil, who has lived with a gun in one hand and an ax in the other, and breasted unnumbered perils, may become, almost in a twinkling of an eye, a first-class soldier. Inured to fatigue, a stranger to the luxuries of life, he can make forced marches, and will soon learn to handle the fire-arms which modern science has perfected, and to face the foe with the coolness of a veteran. The United States have at their disposal this admirable *personnel* whenever it is needed.

The question was asked some years ago of that Frenchman who has, perhaps, most clearly analyzed the Jacobin spirit, "What were the successive changes of sentiment which transformed the veterans of 1792 into the men of 1800?" He replied, "This question can only be answered in closely following their private correspondence. Wholly devoted to the nation, and finding 'in their vocabulary no such word as fail,' their cry of '*ca ira*' reaches the Alpine glaciers. When the reign of terror comes, the most intrepid in the ranks dares not look behind him toward his home. To his eyes the enemy is the only object; all else is unknown or forgotten. Then, after passing the crisis and surmounting the danger, he soon becomes weary of glory and feels a contempt for everything but the army. There is his universe; outside of it is nothing. The army is his all in all, and in it he sees nothing but the General-in-chief. Henceforth nothing of the citizen will remain. The profession absorbs the man; the military spirit absorbs the hero." [1]

The American volunteer has never undergone such transformations. Four years of uninterrupted

1 The "Revolution," by Edgar Quinet, Vol. 2, p. 310 *et seq.*

war did not alter his essential characteristics. He
is a member of the political society of the nation,
and in fighting to maintain it remains deeply
attached to its institutions. Undoubtedly, a spirit
of obedience and discipline gradually prevailed in
the ranks, but without in any wise impairing his in-
dividuality or modifying his political convictions.
He makes war because he belongs to the country,
yet he knows that his is not the profession of arms.
The camp does not blot out the memory of his boy-
ish and youthful habits and associations, nor wean
him from them, and when the war is over he
resumes them without regretting the adventurous
life in which for a time he was engaged.

It is probable that the historian who will some
day recount these facts will be less struck by the
formation of the American armies than by what
took place at the close of the civil war. It was
less difficult to arm a million of men than, at a
later period, to discharge them and send them to
their homes. He will doubtless dwell at length upon
the spirit which animated the masses, but neither
should he overlook the stern control that the Secretary of War exercised over men and events.
The great patriot kept an incessant watch over any
untoward symptoms which might appear in the
Union armies. He taught both officers and soldiers
that their generals were but agents of the civil
power. When men of pre-eminent ability and

12

great vigor of character are called in similar circumstances to the head of affairs, they may, to a certain point, give a direction to events. It rests with them to save republican liberty or to let it perish.

The naval and the military service of the Union are organized very much upon the same principles. Some vessels are in commission to protect the maritime and commercial interests of the republic in time of peace. They are commanded by a select corps of officers, whose number greatly exceeds the habitual requirements of the service; the reason of this being that at any given moment the commercial can be suddenly transformed into a naval marine. In such an eventuality the United States will have at least a portion of the *personnel* for the command of these improvised fleets.

As may be seen, the American people, assuming the defensive, and determined to avoid as far as possible all foreign complications, consider themselves as beyond the reach of invasion, because they are conscious of their ability, at any required moment, to make an immense effort. They may justly rely upon their own vigorous qualities and the mechanical and industrial resources of their country. Doubtless, the actual geographical position of the United States is extremely favorable to this state of things. Since the commencement of their national existence they have beheld the gradual

giving away of the various parts of the European co-
lonial edifice. On the other hand Europe is more
and more impressed with the belief that her interests
upon the continent of North America are growing
less, and after several deplorable attempts she seems
to have almost wholly renounced interference in
its affairs. The federal government has naturally
taken advantage of this state of things; its very
isolation has greatly increased its power of resistance. However, let us for a moment suppose it
surrounded by neighbors; it would, without doubt,
be then obliged to increase its precautionary measures; but were it firmly resolved to maintain
neutrality and abstain from intermeddling with the
concerns of other nations, it would still be possible
to keep on the defensive, and thus become impreg-
nable. Looking to such contingencies, the United
States should require every American to learn to
handle arms. Without even resorting to federal
intervention, each State could undertake this task
and enroll every able-bodied man in the militia, so
that at a given signal the entire nation would be
under arms. If this arrangement prevailed, it
would only remain for the federal government to
keep in reserve a body of general officers capable
of directing operations.

A similar measure might be applied to the naval
forces of the United States; it would suffice to
store in their arsenals material in reserve and

to develop the merchant marine proportionably. Upon any special emergency it would be easy to draw from these elements all needful resources for the defense of the country. Doubtless, these precautions would involve considerable expense; the productive forces of the country would suffer in a certain measure; but what would be such expense compared to that incurred by European societies?

At the same time a methodical organization of the militia would not admit the growth of a spirit of conquest or the birth of a military rule. These defensive precautions would not then affect republican institutions. However, it must here be observed that free America, in spite of the spirit that animates her, could not endure more. Keeping on foot great standing armies never fails to undermine the most solid institutions; little by little a warlike spirit would make its way, and, in proportion to its increase, endanger even the republic itself. The time would come when it might govern the executive and compel the Legislature to come to terms. These contingencies eminently demand the attention of those countries that desire to try the experiment of a republic. Military establishments were created in Europe when royalty gained the ascendant, and they were in perfect harmony with it. By their agency most of the modern nations have attained their development, and now, if monarchical institutions are destined to pass away, standing armies will probably disappear with them.

ADMINISTRATION OF FINANCES.

The history of the financial policy of the United States cannot be given here. It would require long explanations, and withdraw attention from the subjects which this volume was designed to treat.

The policy of neutrality, rendering unnecessary a large military establishment, exercised a decisive influence over financial measures. It is easy to prove this from official documents, all of recent date. When the war of secession broke out, it is nearly the precise truth to say that the Northern States had neither army nor navy. Their fiscal system, organized to meet the very limited exigencies of the government, worked in a very restricted circle. In 1861 every thing had to be at once created. But the majority of the American people were determined to save the Union, and, having once taken this resolution, would not be deterred by any sacrifice. So the levies of men succeeded each other for four years with unexampled rapidity; large and increasing demands for money were constantly made. The nation responded to both. It is proper to add that on repeated occasions in the darkest days of the war, states and cities addressed remonstrances to the federal government, complaining of its extreme caution and its failure to resort to more aggressive measures, and almost always closing by renewed offers of assistance.

These observations serve to facilitate a comprehension of the financial operations of this period. A table of the expenditures, including the interest paid on the debt,[1] is herewith subjoined:

1861 ....$ 66,571,328
1862   474,744,777
1863   714,709,997
1864   865,234,087
1865 1,290,308,982
1866   520,750,939
1870   309,553,560

These figures would be incomplete without adding

1. The federal debt prior to the war, $76,455,299.

2. The sum total of debt contracted by the federal government, say $2,412,547,181.

3. Pensions paid and still payable to the wounded and to the widows and children of deceased soldiers, say $30,000,000 per annum.

4. Finally, the extraordinary expenditures of states, counties, townships and towns on account of the war, amounted, by the most reliable estimates, to $923,000,000. This last item, not being charged to the federal government, is merely alluded to. Thus the United States had, properly speaking, no financial precedents to guide them in providing for these enormous outlays. Before the war they enjoyed, in this respect, an exceptional

---

[1] See the learned reports of Mr. David A. Wells, Special Commissioner of the Revenue, from 1866 to 1870.

position. They were but slightly in debt, and the sums they needed were collected without scarcely exciting public attention. It was natural that questions of finance should be then regarded with but little interest. In 1861 the country entered upon an entirely new state of things, and resolved without hesitation to be equal to it; but in erecting an immense edifice, required for immediate use, more attention was given to its rapid construction than to the adjustment of its proportions. The government acted with promptness and vigor, and the taxes levied from time to time to keep pace with its constantly increasing necessities were cheerfully paid. The working of the system which was adopted subjected to severe trials the patriotism and the power of a people who never sunk under the weight of these burdens.

The two principal sources of revenue during the war were, 1, the internal revenue, composed of taxes intended to reach, under every possible form, all articles of production and consumption ; 2, the duties on merchandise imported into the United States. A table of the prodigious results obtained is here given:

1. Internal revenue:

1863, year of its creation	$ 37,640,787
1864	109,741,134
1865	209,464,215
1867	309,226,813
1867 [1]	266,027,537

1 After a reduction of over $50,000,000, made in consequence of a legislative measure of July 13, 1866.

Finally, in 1870, after new reductions exceeding $80,000,000, the internal revenue still produced $185,128,859.[1]

2. The principles relative to the existing customs duties were established by the act of March 2, 1861. Since its passage, until that of July 14, 1870, the tariff was a dozen times amended. From 1865 to 1868 the average of such duties was raised to 48 per cent. A table of revenue derived therefrom is subjoined:

1861	$39,582,125
1862	49,056,397
1863	69,059,642
1864	102,316,152
1865	84,928,260
1866	179,046,651
1867	176,417,810
1870	194,538,374

It is to be remarked that these duties have not been reduced in proper proportion to the internal revenue tax. The manufacturing interest persuaded the country that duties on imported merchandise were not so onerous on the masses as other taxes, so that, in place of ceasing with the war, the ascending scale continued up to 1870. If we ask why this financial policy succeeded, we must in the first place attribute it to the patriotism of Americans who never despaired of their country. In the second place, the natural riches of almost an entire

1 In 1872 new reductions took place.

continent inspired the confidence of the people, and enabled them to meet the almost crushing demands made upon them. In the third place, there are no unoccupied classes in the United States. Labor is almost always considered honorable, and the rich claim no repose. So that all the living forces of society are perpetually active. And, in conclusion, the American people knew how to put forth great efforts, and after obtaining success, to make a sudden halt. The victory was scarcely won when the executive disbanded the armies and replaced the fleets of the Union on a peace footing; so that expenses immediately diminished, and labor, returning to its former channels of agriculture, industry and commerce, swelled the producing strength of the country. This point cannot be too earnestly insisted upon. The earliest practicable disbandment of the troops enabled the American republic to avoid the grave financial embarrassments which would have inevitably occurred if it had been constrained to keep a large armed force in time of peace. In proof of this assertion, the following table, showing the annual cost of the army and navy from 1861 to 1871, is appended:

	ARMY.	NAVY.
1861	$23,001,530	$12,387,156
1862	394,368,407	42,674,569
1863	599,298,600	63,211,105
1864	690,791,842	85,733,292
1865 [1]	1,031,323,360	122,567,776

[1] It was from the month of June, 1865, that the disbanding commenced.

1866	$284,479,701	$43,324,118
1867	95,224,415	31,034,011
1870	57,655,674	21,780,229
1871 [1]	28,488,194	20,045,417

These figures scarcely require comment; it is evident that, if the army and navy had not been speedily restored to their minimum force, not only would it have been impossible to reduce the debt, but it must have been necessarily increased.

Nevertheless, it cannot be said that the United States could not then have followed an entirely different policy. At the close of the war the French army still occupied Mexico, and many Americans were of opinion that the United States ought to expel it from the country. The attitude of England during the civil war had also given birth to the most bitter feelings, and grave complications seemed almost inevitable. It was the glory of the then Secretary of State to resist all these influences. Mr. Seward retained for diplomatic discussion those questions that other eminent public men desired to settle by the sword. He avoided every cause for war, and preferred to its hazards and sufferings a policy of peace and reparation.

Thus the system of neutrality has given to the whole American administration its peculiar character. To the Presidents of the United States is in great part due the credit of having advanced and maintained these ideas of government. They have

1 Estimate of the Secretary of the Treasury.

created nearly all the system; they have conducted the foreign relations of the country; in moments of crisis they have organized either resistance or attack. They have generally evinced more discretion than Congress, and almost always proved themselves to be worthy of the confidence of the people.

DEPARTMENT OF JUSTICE.

By the Constitution the President is required to take care that the laws shall be faithfully executed.

In the discharge of these arduous duties, he is specially aided by a member of the Cabinet, who acts as his legal adviser, and whose relations to the executive branch of the government are of a peculiar character.

The Attorney-general's office, created September 24th, 1787, became, by virtue of an act of June 22d, 1870, the department of justice. The act transferred to that department, and placed under the supervision of the Attorney-general, who is its chief, all the law-officers who had been previously attached to the other departments. He can refer all questions of law submitted to him, except such as involve a construction of the Constitution, to any of his subordinates, and require a written opinion thereon, which, if approved by him, has the same force and effect as belong to his own. One of the most distinguished juris-consults who have filled

the place thus defines its duties: " We have seen,"
says Mr. Caleb Cushing, " that the act establishing
the office of Attorney-general expressly imposed on
him two classes of duty ; first, to prosecute all suits
in the Supreme Court, in which the United States is
concerned ; and secondly, to give his advice and
opinion in questions of law to the President and to
the heads of departments.

In the discharge of the second-class of the above-
mentioned duties, the action of the Attorney-general
is quasi-judicial. His opinions officially expound
the law in a multitude of cases, where his decision
is, in practice, final and conclusive.

Although the act requiring this duty of the
Attorney-general does not expressly declare what
effect shall be given to his opinion, yet the general
practice of the government has been to follow it ;
partly for the reason that an officer going against it
would be subject to the imputation of disregarding
the law as officially pronounced, and partly from
the great advantage, and almost necessity, of acting
according to uniform rules of law in the management of public business."[1]

However, the head of the department of justice
has not the powers of a quasi-appellate tribunal.
An appeal does not lie to him from another department by a party assuming to be aggrieved by its
action and seeking to have it reviewed. He

[1] Opinions of Attorneys-general, pp. 333-4, Vol. VI.

advises a department on the request of its chief, and only in cases actually depending, in which the United States has an interest. It is impossible for Congress to foresee and specifically provide for all the possible future contingencies of executive business, either in respect to the business itself or the manner of conducting it. In the nature of things, a necessary discretion as to all such business must exist somewhere, and that discretion, when the law does not speak, resides with the President. It stops when the law defines what is to be done by a given head of department, and how he is to do it; but if the law requires an executive act to be performed without saying how or by whom, it must be for the President to supply the defect in virtue of his powers under the Constitution. Sometimes the laws are obscure or abound in conflicting provisions. In all such cases the President may require the advice of the Attorney-general, and it will, in general, be considered as binding. So far as executive action is concerned it is final and beyond the revisory power of the courts.[1] .

The latter have uniformly and firmly refused to interfere, either by mandamus or injunction, with an executive officer in the discharge of duties confided to him by law, and involving the exercise of judgment and discretion. It is proper to add that they will in some cases pass upon his acts,

---

[1] Opinions of the Attorneys-general, Vol. VI. p. 326, *passim.*

when founded upon a misconstruction of the law,
after the title has passed from the government and
the question become one of private right between
adversary parties.

We must here notice that the administration
may be viewed in two ways: the executive agent
may allow himself to be controlled by considerations exclusively political; he will then administer
as so many have done on the European continent.
He may doubtless have the best intentions, hold the
public interest in view, even contribute to the
well being of those under his jurisdiction; and
yet, although personally devoted to political liberty,
his modes of thought will be fatal to the cause he
desires to serve. In free countries, on the contrary,
the functionary should give an entirely different
bent to his ideas. He would thus gradually cease to
be pre-occupied by merely political, and become
more and more influenced by legal considerations.
Then he would conclude that individuals ought to
assert their own claims and rights, and as cases arise
he would confine himself to the duty of interpreting and applying the law. Above all, in peaceful
times he would almost cease to be an administrator
and become in some sense a judge.[1]

In the United States, in the ordinary practice,
those who possess authority act in general very

[1] These remarks neither apply to the intervention of federal
agents in the affairs of the political party to which they belong,
nor to their action in electoral campaigns.

little. Their principal function consists in deciding
what the law authorizes and what it forbids. A
European who should enter the office of the chief of
an executive department would doubtless be aston-
ished to see him less occupied in impressing his
views of public questions on the minds of the subordinates in that branch of the public service over
which he presides, than in deciding matters of law;
and yet this is his principal duty. If he declines
to abide by his own judgment, or wishes to avoid
responsibility, he submits to the Attorney-general
the difficulties he hesitates to solve. In this way
he contracts vastly better habits. He ceases to be
restless and turbulent, and is no longer anxious to
meet all contingencies. He does not look upon
himself as called upon to make a people happy.
The greater part of the time he remains inactive,
until a question is presented, and then his true
functions commence. A kind of *executive magistrate*, he weighs arguments and decides. We
cannot dwell too pointedly upon this difference
between the European and the American functionary; it may be found in every institution. The
President of a French, Italian or German assembly,
for instance, considers himself in many respects as
a sort of administrator. He conducts the deliberations, interferes incessantly, and in short is, or
thinks he is, a political power. The presiding
officer of an American legislative body allows each

one to exercise his own initiative. When there is a conflict of opinion on any question of order, one of the members asks him to pass upon the controverted point. He then examines the precedents and gives his decision. Any dissenting member may appeal from it to the House, and its vote finally settles the question. Thus has been formed that great parliamentary law which for nearly a century has guaranteed the liberty of American legislatures and the rights of those who belong to them.

These observations will aid us in understanding in what manner the President of the United States performs his daily duties. In administrative questions he leaves the citizen almost entire liberty; allows him the initiative; he remains, as far as possible, in a passive position; he is, according to a common expression, the chief magistrate of the country, a title which particularly well describes the head of a republican government.

As may be understood from the explanations already given, the President wields an immense power. As it is incumbent on him to propose general measures to Congress, to furnish it with all the information it requires, and to aid it in elaborating the laws; so he, in a great measure, gives direction to federal legislation. At the same time the Constitution enjoins upon him the execution of the laws. Hence, the necessity of his exercising, in the last resort, the right of interpretation.

In the history of the United States, the action of the executive is everywhere felt. As stated in a preceding page, it has, by skillfully maintaining their foreign policy, essentially aided in securing an almost complete disarmament. It is also due in great part to its firmness and perseverance that the financial system of the country has been upheld. At the same time, numerous precedents are recorded in each branch of the executive administration. We cannot here speak of the personal character of the men who have in succession occupied the presidential chair. History has already given an assured immortality to some of them. Others will be placed in the category of ordinary men. The influence of the latter has, however, been rarely disastrous, as most of them were surrounded by distinguished advisers, who concealed from public view and supplied the personal insufficiency of their chiefs. It is well also to observe that the executive administration has its traditions, for the most part so firmly established that a President can rarely depart from them. A demagogue, entering the White House after having pledged himself to a course contrary to that of his predecessors, (and this is scarcely probable), would soon be constrained to conform to pre-existing usages. It is doubtful if the will of any man, however obstinate, would not bend under the weight of long-settled precedents.

13

At the same time a sentiment of responsibility, inseparable from power, has had the most propitious influence upon the Presidents. They have in general followed the path which duty and honor prescribe and shunned the pursuit of a vain popularity. It is worthy of record that public opinion has appreciated and honored their resistance to the passions and excitements of the hour, and recognized that they were guided in so doing by a love for their country and a desire to promote her permanent interests.

CHAPTER VIII.

WHEN the framers of the Constitution rejected the plan of a collective responsibility of the ministry, they could not have provided for the intervention of Congress in certain executive acts without bringing on a conflict of powers.

On the other hand, had the President been invested with the exclusive right to conclude international engagements, the foreign relations of the Union would have escaped all manner of control; had the appointing power been conferred upon him alone, he would have become the absolute head of the civil and military administration.

The convention avoided these difficulties by adopting a new method; the Senate was clothed with the right of assisting the President as an executive council. The Constitution says, that he " shall have power, by and with the advice and consent of the Senate, to make treaties, provided two-thirds of the Senators present concur,"[1] and that the consent of that body is necessary to

1 Constitution, Article II., Section 2.

the appointment of functionaries nominated by him. These constitutional provisions confer on the Senate prerogatives, which constitute it a council of the government.

We must carefully notice that the Senate, when acting in this special capacity, ceases to be a part of the legislative power. When engaged upon questions of this nature it is, according to a technical expression, transacting "executive business."

It would be difficult to contrive a more satisfactory combination. The Senate is few in number and renewed by thirds. It thus constitutes a permanent body, and can preserve its traditions; whilst on the other hand, thanks to the intimate relations established with the executive, it participates in matters of the highest moment. Conformably to constant practice, whenever the Senate is engaged in the consideration of "executive" questions, the sittings are secret. This rule is as applicable to-day as it was eighty years ago, whenever nominations are disposed of. The debates, in which the antecedents of the nominee are often reviewed with great freedom and warmth, cannot take place in public. But for some years past the inquiry has been made, whether the same reason applies to the discussion of treaty stipulations. How, it is said, can such a usage be maintained when every legislature in Europe deliberates them in open session. For instance, a convention is concluded between the United States and England. It is considered publicly at London, but with closed doors at Washington. Its scope and bearing can be ascertained from the English parliamentary debates, while those in the Senate are a sealed book.

But hitherto the Senate has very justly refused to modify this regulation. Those who desire its continuance say that in a private session much greater latitude in the expression of opinion upon the conduct of diplomatic affairs and the action of the executive can be indulged, and a more searching examination made of the questions at issue.

As it is important to understand fully the authority of the Senate in acting upon such matters, we shall examine in what manner it intervenes, first, in the ratification of treaties, and then in the appointment of officers nominated by the President.

An international engagement is not binding on the United States, except it be ratified by the Senate. This rule is peremptory and without exception. The President is always subject to the action of the council that the Constitution has associated with him. He cannot therefore make secretly such engagements upon which it has had no information. Thus his functions are limited to negotiating, preparing and drafting the convention. He then communicates it to that body, which has an absolute power to approve, reject or amend it.

Foreign powers have, at times, learned to their cóst the full force of these constitutional provisions. At times it has happened that the President has allowed himself to go too far by consenting, in the hope of influencing the Senate, that the execution of certain treaties should be commenced before that body had considered them. On these occasions, the Senate has often vigorously maintained its rights, and at times even disregarded the stipulations the President had made. This happened, for instance, when the United States purchased the islands belonging to Denmark in the West Indies. By the terms of the project of the treaty, the people of St. Thomas and St. John were to be consulted before a transfer of sovereignty could take place. The Danish government fulfilled its engagements faithfully, and the result of the vote in the islands was favorable to their annexation to the United States. The king absolved his subjects from their oath of allegiance. So that, before the Senate had considered the question, Denmark had done certain irrevocable acts; but, notwithstanding, that body refused to regard itself as concluded by them. Vainly did Denmark attempt to maintain that, according to international law, the Senate was bound, and the honor of the United States at stake. All was useless; the Senate decided that it possessed, under the Constitution, rights that no person could compromise. [1]

---

1 Other similar examples might be cited.

On another recent occasion the Senate directly opposed the executive. Soon after his installation, General Grant signed a treaty stipulating for the annexation of the Dominican Republic, and by a separate protocol entered into personal obligations to exert all his influence to obtain its ratification. He kept his word; he neglected no opportunity of presenting to the Senate the advantages of this addition to the territory of the United States; but all his influence was unable to overcome its opposition.

If the United States were not determined to maintain their policy of neutrality and abstention, the province of the Senate in the ratification of treaties would paralyze all the foreign policy of the government.

A power enters into negotiations with the executive, who is represented by the Secretary of State; when they are closed, a treaty is prepared and communicated to the Senate. That body examines, discusses and rejects it. In making known this result to the power with whom he has been in treaty, the Secretary of State is obliged to allege that he has exhausted all appropriate means in his power to obtain a ratification, but that the Senate differed with him in opinion. He expresses regret, and the matter stops there; he can have no direct control over the Senate. Its decision does not affect his constitutional responsibility, or that of the President.

In some countries subject to parliamentary control, matters take a different course. It is the duty of the minister who has signed a treaty to submit it to the Chambers, and ask for its ratification. If the majority withhold their sanction, he can dissolve the assembly and appeal to the electoral body, and if it sustains the majority against him, he tenders his resignation. Then the power with whom he has been in treaty will be satisfied that he has neglected no means at his command in order to meet his engagements. In the United States nothing of the sort exists. A treaty concluded with the executive does not oblige the Senate, and he has no constitutional means of acting on that body. If it dissents from his opinion and refuses the requested ratification, he can neither dissolve it nor appeal to the people.

Nor is this all; according to the constant usage of the United States other nations can have no relations whatever with its deliberative assemblies. American customs would not suffer the accredited minister of a foreign power to treat directly with the Senate upon matters of the greatest interest. What happens in consequence? Any government negotiating with the United States is placed to some extent in a position of inferiority. When its representative signs an engagement, an obligation to have it ratified in due form and by the proper authority is thereby assumed. If a responsible min-

ister makes a treaty, he is bound, if need be, to
dissolve the parliament of his country, or send in
his resignation, if he cannot perform that obligation. On the contrary, as soon as the President
sends the convention to the Senate his power is exhausted, and if that body does not ratify it his responsibility is completely released.

In order to avoid the serious perplexity growing
out of such a state of things, several Presidents, before concluding negotiations, have preferred to
communicate certain projects of treaties to the Senate, for the purpose of consultation, and to ascertain
if it would eventually consent to their ratification.
The executive has in this way always been able to
regulate its action and escape embarrassment and
responsibility.

This was particularly the case in a recent circumstance. When the question relating to the settle-
ment of the Alabama claims became involved with
that of indirect damages, they proposed at London
to negotiate a supplementary treaty, disposing of
this subject. General Grant, having reasons to
doubt if the Senate would authorize him to proceed
further, communicated the project previously to
that body. They modified it in some particulars,
and informed him that negotiations might proceed
on that basis. After past experience, at times so
painful to the powers that have been in treaty with
the United States, it is probable that the method

pursued in regard to this supplementary treaty will be more and more adopted in the future. It has some objectionable features; it is especially almost impossible to guard secresy; but on the other hand it provides against the ultimate disagreement of the Senate, and enables the executive to act with a full knowledge of all the facts bearing on the subject-matter.

The negotiators may also take a middle course and attempt to ascertain in advance, and confidentially, the views and intentions of the principal Senators, so that a satisfactory form may be given to pending negotiations; but this plan requires the utmost tact to ensure success, and is, moreover, liable to be frustrated by those sudden changes of opinion that occur so unexpectedly in all ,deliberative bodies.

However that may be, when the project of a treaty, or a treaty itself, is once decided on or concluded, the President transmits it to the Senate, accompanied by an explanatory message, and very often by papers sustaining it, as for instance the diplomatic correspondence that took place during the negotiations. When these documents are sent to that body it goes into secret session, and on motion of the chairman of the committee on foreign relations the whole subject is referred to that committee. As is known, the Senate committees are organized permanently. Every two years, when

the partial renewal of the assembly takes place,
they are remodeled, but their formation is never
entirely changed. A tradition is thus preserved in
each of them. This is particularly the case with
the committee on foreign relations; it has generally
consisted of distinguished Senators, and most of the
time has had for chairman a statesman of commanding ability. It suffices to mention the names
of Mr. John Forsyth and Mr. Charles Sumner as
proof of the jealous care with which the Senate
has at certain periods chosen those to whom such
delicate and important functions are confided. Under
their auspices and by their labors—and in these past
years this remark applies with special emphasis to
Mr. Sumner—this committee has performed a most
conspicuous part in the history of the foreign affairs
of the Union. In the crises through which the
United States has passed, it has greatly contributed to maintain the foreign policy founded by
Washington; and if at times the executive seemed
inclined to go too far, it has restrained and arrested
his action, so that by the side of the Department of
State is a superintending power which has almost
always saved the country from the fatal effects which
might have resulted from yielding to temporary
excitement.

As soon as the project of a treaty is referred to
the committee on foreign relations, the text and
accompanying papers are printed, and the investi-

gation of the questions is proceeded with. If they
are of importance, the committee very often does
not confine itself to the communications received,
but calls for further information, or even requests
the personal attendance of the Secretary of State
for consultation and a full interchange of views,
and then the subject in all its aspects and bearings
is carefully examined. When the committee is
fully informed it adopts one of the following plans:
it makes a report in favor of the treaty, or proposes amendments, or decides against the ratification; or, without expressing any opinion, submits
the question for the consideration and action of the
Senate; or still again, it allows the time in which
the ratifications are to be exchanged, to expire
without making a report. The Senate can of
course always insist upon a report, but in most
cases great latitude is allowed the committee.

If the committee reports favorably, it generally
looks to the chairman to sustain its opinion. He
is then, in an accommodated sense, a representative
of the executive before the Senate, and an exponent
of the policy of the administration. But if the
majority of the committee oppose the ratification,
he is simply their organ.

As a general thing, party spirit does not enter
largely into foreign questions; they are usually
considered and decided on their own merits. So
the relative strength of parties in the Senate does

not determine the fate of a diplomatic convention. Thus a ratification becomes possible ; were it otherwise, it could not be expected in the majority of cases that two-thirds of the Senators present would vcte in favor of a treaty. If the Senate approve the ratification of the instrument submitted to it, it gives its "advice and consent to the President." He is then authorizéd to set his hand and cause the seal of the United States to be affixed; but he is in no wise obliged to do so, and, if he has changed his opinion, he may always refuse his consent. But when he has given it, the treaty then becomes obligatory upon the United States, and in the energetic words of the Constitution, is an integral part of "the supreme law of the land." However, in 1795, the question arose whether the House of Representatives, in which all bills for raising revenue must originate, was constitutionally bound to vote the money stipulated by an international act to be paid. The biographer of Washington has thus narrated what took place on the occasion of the treaty that John Jay had just concluded with England :

"The Constitution declaring a treaty, when made, the supreme law of the land, it became essentially the duty of the President officially to announce it to the people of the United States. In pursuance of this duty he issued his proclamation dated the last day of February.........For the information of

Congress, a copy of this proclamation was transmitted to each House on the first of March........."

" The party which had attained the majority in one branch of the Legislature, having openly denied the right of the President to negotiate a treaty of commerce, was not a little dissatisfied at his venturing to issue this proclamation before the sense of the House of Representatives.had been declared on the obligation of the instrument."

" This dissatisfaction was not concealed. On the second of March Mr. Livingston........laid upon the table a resolution requesting the President ' to lay before the House a copy of the instructions, ...together with the correspondence and other documents, relative to said treaty.'........The debates soon glided into an argument on the nature and extent of the treaty-making power."

" By the friends of the administration it was maintained that a treaty was a contract between two nations, which, under the Constitution, the President, by and with the advice and consent of the Senate, had a right to make, and that it was made when, by and with such advice and consent, it had received its final act. Its obligations then became complete on the United States........."

" By the opposition it was contended that the powers to make treaties, if applicable to every object, conflicted with powers which were vested exclusively in Congress. That either the treaty-making power must be limited in its operation so as not to touch objects committed·by the Constitution to Congress, or the assent and co-operation of the House of Representatives must be required to give validity to any compact, so far as it might comprehend those objects. A treaty, therefore, which required an appropriation of money or any act of Congress to carry it into effect, had not acquired its obligatory force until the House of Representatives had exercised its powers in the case. They were at full liberty to make or withhold such appropriation, or other law........."

" The debate........was protracted without intermission until the 22d of March, when the resolution was carried in the affirmative by sixty-two to thirty-seven voices.".........(22d March, 1795.) " The situation in which this vote placed the executive was peculiarly delicate........He returned the following answer to the resolution which had been presented to him........' To admit then a right in the House of Representatives to demand, and to have, as a matter of course, all the papers respecting a negotiation with a foreign power, would be to establish a dangerous precedent.' "........." The course which the debate has taken on the resolution of the House," adds Washington, " leads to some observations on the mode of making treaties under the Constitution of the United States." [1]

1 Life of Washington, by John Marshall, Vol. V., p. 650 *et seq.*

The President then reminded them that he had been a member of the convention; that it had intended to confer the treaty-making power on the executive alone, with the advice and consent of two-thirds of the Senators present; that every treaty negotiated and ratified in this manner ought to become binding; and the message adds, that the House of Representatives, up to that time, had consented to and accepted this interpretation of the fundamental law; so Washington refused to send the papers asked for. The House, in reply to this message, adopted resolutions re-affirming its right. The debate continued, and was assuming proportions of greater magnitude, when a member proposed to vote the measures necessary for the execution of the treaty. The House finally understanding that resistance was useless, passed, the 29th of April following, by a small majority, the law which put into execution the treaty concluded with England. [1]

Since, then, this same question of constitutional right has been raised from time to time. Quite recently on the occasion of the cession of Alaska, the House of Representatives again assumed that the President and the Senate could not bind the action of Congress; however, after a somewhat animated debate, the concession was finally made, and the necessary sums voted in payment to Russia.

[1] Life of Washington, by John Marshall, Vol. V., p. 555 *et seq.*

An experience of nearly a century proves that the Senate has generally been very moderate; that its policy has been rather timid than bold; that it has restrained more than it has urged forward the Executive Power. In a word, it has very often exercised a control, all the more salutary, because in a republic there is much greater peril in acting on foreign questions than in keeping on the defensive. Indeed when we examine the progressive development of democratic ideas, it will readily be seen that they cannot harmonize with the combinations of diplomatic policy. Secret alliances and projects, whose execution can only be slowly matured, are either unknown, or repugnant, to societies in which those ideas prevail. They dread entering into engagements, and ought to avoid compromising themselves. The complicated mechanism of a negotiation that proceeds through two distinct phases, is not distasteful to them. This mode affords them protection, and the executive can neither compromise nor pledge the country. On the other hand we have only to examine the international alliances concluded by the United States, to perceive that the intervention of the Senate has often been most advantageous. At the same time if it be true, as Americans believe, that a system of ministerial responsibility is incompatible with the very existence of the republic, legislatures certainly should not be vested with the power of granting or withholding consent to the

14

ratification of treaties. It necessarily follows that the President must have near him a governmental council.

The inquiry has been made whether it would be preferable to disconnect this council from the legislative assemblies? But why, it is said in reply, add to the machinery of the Constitution? Again, without here investigating how far the Senate gains by this combination, does not the executive derive from it great advantages, and may not the country place entire confidence in the control that this body exercises over the foreign affairs of the Union?

In what manner does the Senate intervene in the nomination of public functionaries?

The President is the head of the executive administration; he gives his orders; it is his duty to take care that his agents in their respective spheres of action fulfill the mission confided to them. However, if we examine American legislation, it is to be remarked, that as a general thing public officers are not to be political agents; in effect, if we except the foreign representatives of the United States, we find in the administration the members of the magistracy and treasury agents; the officers connected with the mail, pension, public land, Indian and patent service; those appointed to the territories and finally the army and the navy officers. The federal power, then, properly speaking, sends no political representatives among the people. However, the force of circumstances has so greatly changed this provision of the law, that the collectors of customs have become in fact the depositaries of the ideas and purposes of the government, and postmasters give as much attention to the elections as to the service of the mails.

In this way the administration has become quite different from what was originally designed by its framers. Doubtless, we ought not to be surprised at what has actually taken place. A government cannot exist without political agents, and proportionably with its development the exigencies of the situation bear so heavily on it that it requires to be represented among the people, to be placed in contact with them, and, in a word, to act upon them; and the state organizations cannot serve as a medium to effect this. In the course of this investigation we shall see how those independent autonomies are brought into relations with the Executive Power, and in what manner and within what limits it may interpose; but these intervening relations are not sufficient to assure to the government the strength it needs.

Impelled by the urgency of these demands, the treasury agents and other officials dependent on the executive departments, have gone beyond the limits of their appropriate and legitimate sphere of duty. If, meanwhile, we look into the manner of appointing them, it is easier to understand why they are almost irresistibly led to interest themselves in politics. There is no administrative hierarchy in the United States. A functionary is for the most part selected almost at random, and he knows that he will not remain long in office. The idea of a strongly organized civil service, such as exists in Germany, for instance, or in certain branches of the French financial administration, has not yet reached the American mind. But we must not, however, conclude that the President is free to give public offices to those in whom he has the most confidence; on the contrary, the persons from whom his selections are made, form, in fact, rather a small circle. He is constrained to resort to the politicians, and among them he recruits the office-holders. If now what has already been said regarding party organization be recalled, it is easy to see how things are managed. In the primary meetings, heretofore mentioned, some leaders prepare the success of a candidate, and it would be difficult for him to refuse to reward their services. In the national convention it usually happens that a small number of politicians will control the nomination of the candidate for President, which the electors will ratify at a later day. When he is elected, those who have so greatly contributed to his success will naturally have a right to his grateful recognition, and even if we admit that no previous agreement existed, how can he overlook such assistance? In this way he will have, in most cases, made his selections in advance.

In the United States *politicians*, as a class, are much maligned, but it is impossible to govern without their aid; if amongst them are corrupt men, there are also others, who render eminent service to their country. Good and evil are therefore so blended that it is difficult to foresee the effect on American politics of a radical reform of existing customs. However that may be, in the first stage of party organization, as in national conventions, the same system is found; the same ideas of patronage prevail. Hence arises the maxim, almost savage in its brutality—"to the victors belong the spoils."

On account of the influence which it gives, patronage is in general sought for with avidity by Senators and Representatives in Congress. This renders the position of the President difficult. He nominates for public offices, but he can scarcely be said to have freedom of choice, for he has not only to reward those who have served him, but also to regard the wishes expressed by members of Congress and the necessities of their position. Mr. Lincoln was one day asked by one of his sincere and devoted friends—"Who is President, you or A?" This is what led to this strange question: A had, as a strict Republican, energetically sustained the policy of the administration in the House of Representatives, and at the commencement of the presidency of Mr. Lincoln had pressed the appointment of B as postmaster of the most important place of his district. B was an honest man and a good citizen, and the choice was therefore a fortunate one. He became an excellent *employé*. His politics remained unchanged, and he spared no effort to aid the prosecution of the war. He was popular with the people of the town, the Postmaster-general approved his conduct, and even his political adversaries did not complain of him. But he made one fatal mistake; he did not pay sufficient deference to A; he even went so far as to criticise one or two of his speeches, disapprove two of his votes, and state that he would no longer 'support him. So soon as A was apprised of these facts, he went immediately to the President and asked B's dismissal. "I must do it," said Mr. Lincoln to the friend to whom he confided his embarrassment. " I regret it exceedingly, but it cannot be helped." His friend then inquired, " Who is President, you or A ? " " A is President," answered Mr. Lincoln.

This great patriot then explained to his friend that everything must be made to yield to the necessities of the war; that he must not weaken his administration; that it was better that he should be accused of weakness than alienate members of Congress ; that he must at every cost avoid a division of those forces which the government so greatly needed. Unfortunately the situation remains unchanged, although the urgent necessities of that period no longer exist. The system now in force may thus be described : Those districts represented in Congress by faithful Republicans— that is to say, by Republicans who sustain the administration, so long as it does their bidding— belong to them, and they dispose of its patronage. The districts that send Democrats, or opponents of the administration, are controlled by the Senators of the State, if they support the administration. When it occurs that the Representatives of a district and the Senators from the State are both of the opposition, the patronage reverts to the President and his Cabinet. Such is the custom, and if the executive is not disposed to comply with it, he excites the most violent discontent.

When General Grant entered upon the office of President he had made no engagements with the party leaders [1] who had elected him. It might have been supposed that he would seek to restore to the executive authority its ancient and unfettered right to nominate for public offices. But the practice of bestowing patronage had taken such deep root that he soon perceived that such an attempt would be unavailing. He was then obliged to yield to the usage and follow the example of his prede-

1 See " The Nation," No. 370, August 1, 1872.

cessors. Abuses necessarily became more alarming as the necessities of the war had developed in the country an administrative force of greater numbers and strength. An evil which might be tolerated when there were but few office-holders, became insupportable when their number reached nearly sixty thousand.

How far would the adoption by the United States of the administrative rules enforced in other countries modify the situation? Would the formation of a civil hierarchy be compatible with a free democracy? It would be impossible as yet to say. There is an evident and pressing necessity for an entire change in the present state of things; but up to the present time no one has discovered an efficacious means of suppressing this disorder. However that may be, Congress should first be forced to return to its allotted sphere of duty, and to renounce the patronage which exercises over it so corrupting an influence, and the President especially should regain the exercise of one of his essential prerogatives. As the "Federalist" said, "the true test of a good government is its aptitude and tendency to produce a good administration." Now how can this be attained when the executive agents are not really the men of his choice, and he is forced to submit to the wishes and caprices of members of Congress?

The framers of the Constitution intended to

reserve to the executive the power to choose the
functionaries of the government; the intervention
of the Senate was expected to give greater stability
to the administration. Thus the constitutional
provision was intended not so much to guard against
any possibly bad selections by the President, as
to build up a certain order of things.[1]

However, at that period grave objections were
made against the co-operation of the Senate with
the President. Some asserted that it would lead
him to exercise an undue influence over the Senate; others, that the Senate would intrench upon
his functions. Hamilton met these strictures
by a well-known process of reasoning. He said
that these two arguments destroyed each other.
But he was for once mistaken, for both are equally
well founded. The history of the relations between
the President and the Senate actually shows that
he almost always uses his patronage to secure a
majority in that body, and that it invades his do-
main by forcing upon him its applicants for public
offices. Lamentable disorder is the result, and although the Constitution wisely surrounded him
with an executive council, it is none the less certain that hitherto it has been impossible to separate
exactly his personal privileges from those of his
council. In ordinary practice, as the opposition
is not considered, the Senators who belong to the

---

[1] The " Federalist," p. 529 *et seq.*

majority may, in regard to the question of offices, be classed in two divisions. There are some whose secure personal position renders them indifferent to patronage; but there are others who can only succeed in sustaining themselves by a skillful distribution of it. The latter are usually ready to support all the measures of, the administration, less from conviction than a desire to propitiate the favor of the President. Hence a continual exchange of good offices between him and them. They give their votes and dispose of appointments, so that, by an abuse arising from an easily recognized cause, an unscrupulous Senator imposes humiliating conditions on a President, who cannot readily dispense with his support. In this way constitutional provisions regarding a choice of functionaries are in part evaded; the executive loses the strength and freedom of the initiative which the fundamental law designed to give him. The Senate, on the other hand, loses its independence; the duties enjoined upon it as his council are measurably shorn of their importance, and it at the same time forgets or disregards its legislative functions.

This difficult subject has engaged the attention of the best minds of the country for some years past, and they have found, as they suppose, the solution of the problem. The method which they recommend is:

1. To create a civil hierarchy.

2. To forbid office-holders attending to politics, and especially taking an active part in electoral campaigns.

It is certain that when an administration could be recruited from its own ranks there would be no longer any reason for "dividing the spoils" after each election; a body of officials would be formed animated by the proper spirit and interested in their duties. The President would select from them those who best merit advancement, and would be guided by fixed rules in so doing. Then it would only remain for the Senate to exercise a kind of general supervision.

Such a reform would doubtless put an end to the most crying abuses of the system now in force. These changes seem to be very desirable, with reference to the upright and efficient management of public affairs and to the political morality of the country, and yet they can not be advocated without some uneasiness. It is easy to tell how a good administration may be formed, but it is not so easy to foresee how far a permanent hierarchy would be compatible with the existence of great political parties.

No matter how free a democracy may be supposed, there is always among certain classes of the people a feeling of indifference to public affairs, and political absenteeism has to be incessantly combatted.

Now the great skill of parties is shown in keeping the interest of the masses constantly aroused,
and when election day arrives to induce them to
go to the polls. What will be the effect of removing the powerful motive that contributes so much
to excite their action, by destroying the interests
which a hope of office keeps alive? Is it not
to be feared that a contest for principles alone will
not suffice to hold together all the elements of a
political organization ? If, then, the creation of an
administrative hierarchy would, as there is reason to
fear, result in a diminution of the public life, it is
evident that the meditated reform, however important from other stand-points, might tend to produce
an irreparable evil. And in this connection, one of
the most complicated problems involved in the organization of free democracies is presented. How is a
nation of forty millions of men to be induced to
give constant attention to public affairs? The
American people have considered these difficulties,
but not solved them. They have instructed their
politicians to form and maintain parties, and confided to them the task of explaining, periodically,
political issues. In fact they have simply reserved
to themselves the sovereign right of deciding between these different organizations thus formed.
Moreover, they have resigned to those active managers, who have secured a favorable popular verdict
for their party, the right of dividing the public

offices between them. If it be now withdrawn there is reason for apprehending that so radical a change will disorganize the whole political machine; so that in applauding the motives of American reformers it is important to know if they have exactly measured the question in its fullest extent, and if their remedy for existing evils would not, if applied, result in impairing the public spirit of the country. These are serious inquiries, to which it would be as yet impossible to give a satisfactory answer.[1]

While we indicate these perplexities, we propose to limit ourselves to the remark, that, according to the Constitution, the executive has the exclusive right of nominating all the functionaries of the United States. Doubtless he could impose such administrative regulations as would organize the civil service upon a plan somewhat analagous to that adopted for the army and navy, but this should only be attempted with great caution—by feeling, as it were, the way at every step—and in such manner as not to destroy the great political parties whose existence may perchance be indispensable to the maintenance of liberty.

And yet, again, the convention acted wisely in placing near the President an executive council authorized to revise and, if necessary, defeat his

1 We would here particularly recommend to the reader a speech that Senator Schurz delivered in the Senate, Jan. 27, 1871, and which was published under the title of " Civil Service Reform."

nominations; but its functions can be usefully exercised only on condition of remaining within the limits assigned to it by the Constitution. It is in fact indispensable that the administrative patronage should no longer be controlled by the legislative bodies, and in particular by the Senate.

In this matter there can be but little doubt; these changes will be made; the most distinguished minds demand them, and sooner or later the popular voice will insist on them. We may then look forward to legislation forbidding, under severe penalties, any member of either house presenting to the President candidates for public offices. As may be seen, this reform would not necessarily imply the creation of an administrative hierarchy; but it would have the double effect of confining Congress to the exercise of its appropriate functions, and of assuring its independence of the executive. At the same time the Senate would freely exercise the control over executive nominations, confided to it by the Constitution.

CHAPTER IX.

IT has been shown, in the preceding chapters, that the framers of the Constitution were in favor of creating a vigorous Executive Power, and making it, as far as possible, independent of the legislative branch of the government. There is no longer any doubt that their conception was just, and that they understood the true nature of republican institutions.

However, the Executive Power, such as they conceived it, would ere long have exceeded its prescribed limits if the independence of the States had been wholly destroyed. It is owing to the constitutional recognition of their existence and authority that a free republic has been upheld in the United States. After an experience of nearly a century, and an expression of concurring opinions by the most distinguished statesmen in favor of maintaining these local governments, it would seem superfluous to an American to insist on this point, or to prove their necessity. Nevertheless, as these ideas are not so fully accepted elsewhere, it may be useful to explain why in the United States the existence of the States is an indispensable safeguard of republican liberty.

"The federal government," says the Supreme Court in a leading case, "proceeds directly from the people; is ordained and established in the name of the people, and is declared to be ordained in order to form a more perfect union, establish justice, ensure domestic tranquillity, and secure the blessings of liberty to themselves and to their posterity. The assent of the States, in their sovereign capacity, is implied in calling a convention, and thus submitting that instrument to the people. But the people were at perfect liberty to accept or reject it, and their act was final. It required not the affirmance and could not be negotiated by the State governments. The Constitution, when thus adopted, was a complete obligation, and bound the State sovereignties.

"The government of the Union, then, is emphatically and truly a government of the people." In form and in substance it emanates from them. Its powers are granted by them, and are to be exercised directly on them, and for their benefit. This government is acknowledged by all to be one of enumerated powers. The principle that it can only exercise the powers granted to it is apparent. ....The Government of the Union, though limited in its powers, is supreme within its sphere of action..........It is the government of all; its powers are delegated by all; it represents all, and acts for all..........But this question is not left to mere reason; the people have, in express terms, decided it by saying, this Constitution and the laws of the United States, which shall be made in pursuance thereof,..........shall be the supreme law of the land, and .the judges in every State shall be bound thereby, anything in the Constitution or laws of any State to the contrary notwithstanding." [1]

Thus the people of the United States constitute a nation placed under one government, but ".........on the other hand the people of each State compose a State, having its own government and endowed with all the functions essential to separate and independent existence. The States disunited might continue to exist. Without the States in union there could be no such political body as the United States........."

".........But in many articles of the Constitution the necessary existence of the States, and within their proper spheres the independent authority of the States, is distinctly recognized. To them nearly the whole charge of interior regulation is committed or left; to them and to the people all powers not expressly delegated to the national government are reserved. The general condition was well stated

1 McCullough *vs* State of Maryland, 4 Wheaton, p. 816 *et seq.*. Decision of Mr. Chief Justice Marshall.

15

by Mr. Madison, in the "Federalist," thus: 'The Federal and State governments are, in fact, but different agents and trustees of the people, constituted with different powers and designated for different purposes.'.........."[1]

The State, on her admission into the Union, surrenders a portion of her sovereignty to the federal government, and in this regard there is no distinction between the original States and those subsequently formed. However, it is important to notice, that this surrender or delegation of power is not made by the State, but really and in fact by the people thereof. It is they who actually decide to enter the Union. They then ratify the division of powers between the federal and the State governments, reserving to themselves all the prerogatives of sovereignty not conferred on either.

It happens in this way that, in their respective spheres, these two organizations have scarcely anything in common. The one is invested with various prerogatives, the exercise of which has been confided to it by the Constitution; each State, considered as an autonomy, exerts, on the contrary, those powers bestowed upon her by her people. This doctrine suggested to President Jackson the following reflections: "The destruction of our State governments, or the annihilation of their control

---

[1] See the decision of the Supreme Court, given by Mr. Chief Justice Chase, in the case of Lane County *vs.* Oregon. See 7 Wallace: and McPherson's Manual for 1869, p. 440 *et seq.*

over the local concerns of the people, would lead directly to revolution and anarchy, and finally to despotism and military domination. In proportion, therefore, as the general government encroaches upon the rights of the States, in the same proportion does it impair its own power."[1]

However, the Constitution declares that "the United States shall guarantee to every State in this Union a republican form of government, and shall protect each of them against invasion; and on application of the Legislature, or of the executive (when the Legislature cannot be convened), against domestic violence."[2]

This article has given rise to long and animated discussions, and the opposing parties are evidently far from agreeing as to its true construction.

The framers of the Constitution thought that a faction might triumph in some one of the States, overthrow its republican institutions, and establish in their stead a monarchy or a despotism; they then foresaw that circumstances might thus occur when the federal government would be rendered powerless. The "Federalist" expressed this apprehension in the following terms: "In a confederacy founded on republican principles and composed of republican members, the superintending government ought clearly to possess authority to defend

1 Inaugural Address, March 4, 1833.. Presidents' Messages, p. 477.
2 Constitution, Article IV., Section 4.

the system against aristocratic or monarchical inno-vations. The more intimate the nature of such a Union may be, the greater interest have the mem-bers in the political institutions of each other, and the greater right to insist that the forms of govern-ment, under which the compact was entered into, should be substantially maintained."[1]

This clause, then, leaves to the people of each State the absolute right to modify the forms of their republican institutions, but forbids them to sub-stitute in their stead such as are monarchical or aris-tocratic. If this prohibition is violated, the federal government should at once intervene. However, this rule of action, which in the abstract seems so clear, has not always been of easy application. For instance, at the period preceding the civil war certain States of the south had modified their "republican institutions" to such an extent as to render them true aristocracies; nevertheless, the federal government never thought of interposing its authority. If it subsequently did so in a very energetic manner, it was only because exceptional circumstances gave it the opportunity. Nor was it, then, in virtue of this clause of the Constitu-tion. It determined to resist by force the secession movement, because the life of the nation was in-volved in the issue. The importance of this guar-antee was only revealed at a later period, when the

[1] The "Federalist," p. 132 *et seq.*

re-establishment of the insurrectionary States in the Union was considered; but this is not the place to present the arguments advanced on either side after the triumph of the federal arms.

In case an insurrection bursts forth in any one of the States, and overthrows a republican form of government, the President should act without delay, as on him would first devolve the task of meeting the danger and re-establishing order. All the forces of the United States are placed at his disposition, and it is his duty to determine the employment that shall be made of them.

Besides, it is difficult to understand the bearing of this guarantee clause without examining the latter part of the section containing it, and consulting the adjudication of the Supreme Court to which it gave rise, under the following circumstances: The abettors of a revolutionary organization in Rhode Island proclaimed it to be the lawfully constituted government of the State, and resorted to force to maintain it against the pre-existing government. Both were in form republican, but the latter continued in the exercise of its functions, suppressed the armed opposition to it, and enforced the due execution of its laws. A suit grew out of some of the proceedings connected with this unfortunate affair, and one of the questions raised was evidently designed to elicit from the court an expression as to which was the rightful government. Mr. Chief Justice Taney delivered the opinion:

".........Moreover, the Constitution of the United States, as far as it has provided for an emergency of this kind, and authorized the general government to interfere in the domestic concerns of a State, has treated the subject as political in its nature, and placed the power in the hands of that department."

"Under this article of the Constitution it rests with Congress to decide what government is the established one in the State. For as the United States guarantees to each State a republican government, Congress must necessarily decide what government is established in the State before it can determine whether it is republican or not. And when the Senators and Representatives of a State are admitted into the councils of the Union, the authority of the government under which they are appointed, as well as its republican character, is recognized by the proper constitutional authority. ....Yet the right to decide is placed there and not in the courts........."

"So, too, as relates to the clause in the above-mentioned article of the Constitution, providing for cases of domestic violence. It rested with Congress to determine upon the means proper to be adopted to fulfill this guarantee.........The act of February 28, 1795, provided that 'in case of an insurrection in any State against the government thereof, it shall be lawful for the President of the United States, on application of the Legislature of such State, or the executive (when the Legislature cannot be convened), to call forth such number of the militia of any other State or States as may be applied for, as he may judge sufficient to suppress such insurrection.'

" By this act the power of deciding whether the exigency had arisen upon which the government of the United States is bound to interfere is given to the President. He is to act upon the application of the Legislature, or of the executive, and consequently he must determine what body of men constitute the Legislature, and who is the Governor, before he can act. The fact that both parties claim the right to the government cannot alter the case, for both cannot be entitled to it. If there is an armed conflict like the one we are speaking of, it is a case of domestic violence, and one of the parties must be in insurrection against the lawful government. And the President must of necessity decide which is the goverment, and which party is unlawfully arrayed against it, before he can perform the duty imposed upon him by the act of Congress."[1]

So that, in affairs of such delicacy, it devolves upon the head of the Executive Power to decide.

The explanations heretofore given of the powers

---

[1] Luther *vs.* Barden, 7 Howard, p. 1 *et seq.*

of peace and war, and the obligations that the defense of the country imposes on the President, suffice to show in what manner the practice under the Constitution has determined the meaning of the second clause of the section.

However, the calling out the militia at the beginning of the civil war raised a very serious question. When President Lincoln issued a proclamation inviting the Governors of the States to furnish their respective portions of the contingent, several among them refused to comply, on the pretense that his call was unconstitutional. But Congress soon put an end to this disorder. The government, having derived its powers, not from the States, but from the people, it appealed directly to the latter, and not to any intervening agency, and provided that, if need be, federal officers in the several States should be appointed with full authority to proceed to a direct recruitment.

Thus, if we do not include the exceptional cases just mentioned, the Union and the States act, if we may say so, in distinct and independent spheres. The President and Congress should abstain from asserting the powers delegated by the people to the local governments. The latter cannot rightfully suspend the national authority or interfere with its exercise. If, then, the government of the United States is not a league or confederacy of States, as separate and sovereign communities united by a

compact, neither is it a consolidated government,
without limitation of powers, representing the
entire sovereignty. It was designed to maintain
not only the supremacy of the national authority,
but also the reserved rights of the States. Federal
encroachments on those rights would be fatal to
republican institutions on this continent.

We may readily see that, should the autonomy
of the States disappear, the Executive Power would
at once essentially change and assume inordinate
proportions. It is to a great extent confined by·
the State governments to that sphere of action prescribed for it by the Constitution. In fact, incessant conflicts would take place between the executive, which is independent within the scope of its
constitutional authority, and the Legislature, with
the increased powers that would almost necessarily
attach to it on the destruction of the governments
of the separate States. From that time one might
foresee that the President, although a person of limited ability, would succeed in gaining the sympathy
and influence of a majority of the people. Doubtless the latter might at times declare in favor of a
deliberative assembly, but it would not be safe to
depend on their permanent support. Called upon to
choose between an abstract sovereignty and the con-
crete idea of power centered in one man, they would
in the end almost always prefer the living personality, and recognize him as the elect of the nation,

without scarcely remembering that they had also chosen their representatives.

The government of the United States is as vigorous as circumstances may require. The executive authority is so constituted that it may act. with perfect liberty within its authorized limits, and these are hedged in by barriers which cannot be readily surmounted. On one side it is confronted by the Legislature and by a firmly established judicial power, which is almost always able to expound and enforce the rights of citizens, and on the other are these thirty-seven independent bodies, which are scarcely amenable to its action. Thanks to this combination, the presidential power is exerted with vigor, and it proves equal to all the requirements of the most varied situations; and nevertheless he to whom it is confided may be, from time to time, changed, because no man is an indispensable necessity. But let the organization of the States disappear, and the condition of things will at once become modified. This was clearly seen in the interval between the overthrow of the Confederate government and the present moment. As is known, Congress decided that the inhabitants of the insurrectionary States had renounced their privileges and power in the Union.[1]

This is not the place to examine the bearing or the character of the measures then adopted, but it

---

[1] Report of the Committee on Reconstruction, p. 11 *et seq.*

is impossible to deny that, by reason of the destruction of these ten States, the federal authority was largely extended beyond its constitutional limits. In fact an immense power was assumed and exercised. If this anomalous state of things had been greatly prolonged, and the dominant party had not labored to efface even the last traces of it, we may be allowed to express the opinion, that there might have resulted a centralized republic, which would with great difficulty have been maintained.

These eventful times also brought about a conflict between the President and Congress. Was the power to reconstruct the Union vested in him or in them? Their respective partisans discussed this preliminary inquiry with equal violence, and the struggle was renewed, when the question arose as to what plan of reconstruction should be adopted. At last matters reached a most critical point. The President was impeached, and narrowly escaped conviction. The momentary disorganization of ten States was enough to endanger the life of the federal government. The equipoise and division of powers so carefully adjusted by the Constitution were deranged, and it seemed that they would be entirely broken up. If the friends of freedom in America did not despair of the republic, it was because of their trust and belief that the conflict would be short, and that the normal and benignant sway of their institutions would be gradually restored.   Let us then hope that the reg-ular action of life will by degrees be resumed and felt in each of the Southern States.   The natural order of things will then be re-established throughout the Union; but until this propitious event occurs, there will be eccentric movements in the working of the federal government, and from time to time threatening attempts at centralization.

CHAPTER X.

THE observations made in the preceding chapters with regard to the prerogatives of the executive would be incomplete without an attempt to explain the transformation they underwent during the civil war. We must remark their sudden expansion, and in what manner those who sustained the executive found means to supply him with all the required resources to resist the attacks which imperiled the existence of the United States.

On the 4th of March, 1861, when Mr. Lincoln delivered his inaugural address, it might have seemed as if the federal government was destroyed. Although the President said, "I consider that the Union is unbroken, and to the extent of my ability I shall take care, as the Constitution itself expressly enjoins upon me, that the laws of the Union be faithfully executed in all the States," he, however, added that he would take no steps that would have the effect to bring on a war; so he

(237)

confined himself to an appeal to misguided citizens, and to a masterly argument to prove that the Constitution interdicted their going out of the Union. Under circumstances of such gravity, never had the head of a government expressed himself with greater reserve nor taken a more modest attitude. He seemed to feel that all the constitutional organization of the United States was on the point of dissolution.

Six weeks later the secessionists fired the first gun at Fort Sumter. The President met this provocation by measures of defense. He immediately called forth 75,000 men under arms, convoked Congress, and declared the blockade of the ports of the South. War was commenced. In reality, in this, the most trying period in the history of the United States, in deciding that the Union should be defended by force of arms, he simply carried into effect the will of the people. Already, for several months, in the midst of the confusion attending the last months of Mr. Buchanan's administration, the Northern States appeared to realize that war was inevitable, and in many respects commenced preparing for it. The politicians, alarmed at impending events, met and tried to effect a compromise. During this time, when the Southern States were preparing to act, contemporary documents prove that the citizens of the North were learning to handle arms, assembling by companies and regiments, and seeking in advance for men to lead them. This, so to speak, preliminary work accounts for what took place in the country from the moment that Mr. Lincoln decided the question and resolved to resist force by force, and explains why the people of the North showed themselves ready to face the crisis.

From the beginning of hostilities, and as a logical sequence of them, all the powers which attach to belligerence inured to the government and were at once called into exercise. A former President of the United States once said in the House of Repre-. sentatives: "There are, then, in the authority of Congress and of the executive, two classes of powers, altogether different in their nature and often incompatible with each other—*the war power and the peace power.* The *peace power* is limited by regulations and restricted by provisions prescribed within the Constitution itself. The *war power* is limited only by the laws and usages of nations. This power is tremendous; it is strictly constitutional, but it breaks down every barrier so anxiously erected for the protection of liberty, of property and of life."

There are, indeed, adds the speaker, *powers of peace* conferred upon Congress which also come within the scope amd jurisdiction of the laws of nations, such as the negotiation of treaties of amity and commerce, the interchange of public ministers

and consuls, and all the personal and social inter-
course between the individual inhabitants of the
United States and foreign nations, and the Indian
tribes, which require the interposition of any law.
But the *powers of war* are all regulated by the laws
of nations, and are subject to no other limitation."[1]

Thus, at the breaking forth of hostilites Mr.
Lincoln was thereby invested with extraordinary powers; and here a constitutional provision
will enable us still better to define his novel situation.   Section II. of article 2 says: "The President
shall be commander-in-chief of the army and navy
of the United States, and of the militia of the several States when called into the actual service of
the United States."   However, these powers were
not exerted without giving rise to violent discussions.   Even among those who scarcely questioned
Mr. Lincoln's right to take all the necessary measures for the reconstruction of the Union and the
provisional administration of the conquered territory many disagreed with him as to whether the
loyal States should be subjected during the continuance of the war to an exceptional *régime*, and as to
his authority to suspend the privilege of the writ
of *habeas corpus*, and try, by military commissions,
citizens accused of political crimes.

And on these points the best minds may readily differ.   The Constitution- had foreseen that

[1] Speech delivered by Mr. John Quincy Adams in the House of
Representatives, 26th May, 1836.

the public necessities might require a suspension of the writ of *habeas corpus*, but does not declare whether in that event Congress alone has the power to authorize it. However, without regarding the precedents which seemed to decide that the whole matter was within the exclusive province of that body, the President, after having consulted the Attorney-general, took the initiative, and issued a proclamation suspending the writ in certain States. A serious contest then arose between him and the judiciary, represented by the Chief Justice of the United States. The latter, in a case pending before him, decided that the measure was illegal, but acknowledged his inability to cause his opinion and judgment to be carried into effect.

In fact, the executive triumphed over the judiciary; but the question regarding the power thus exercised remained in abeyance until March 3, 1863. It was only then that Congress passed an act which sanctioned the then existing state of things. It legalized any arrest or imprisonment during the rebellion which had been made or committed under the authority of the President, and authorized him, whenever in his judgment the public safety might require it, to suspend the privilege of the writ in any case throughout the United States. Reasons in support of this stringent policy were certainly not wanting. Disloyal movements in several of the Northern States urgently required vigilant super-

16

vision, and it was vitally important to check the growth of conspiracies and enforce the execution of the laws.

Considerations of this character led to the organization of military commissions in Indiana and at several other points. However, it is proper to remark that when the question of their validity was brought before the Supreme Court, a majority of the judges held that these extraordinary tribunals had not been, and could not be, legally formed in a State not occupied by the insurgents.[1] But this judgment was not rendered until 1866; so that if it afforded instruction for the future, it could have no retroactive effect.

As regards the States in insurrection, few persons seriously contested the authority of the President. Here then the doctrine relating to the *war power* was applied in its fullest extent; the rights of the conquerors were only limited by international laws and usages. In this way he was able to take decisive steps to abolish slavery.

In his speech of 26th of May, 1836, John Quincy Adams had already shown how abolition measures could be brought about by the theory that he explained, "........ but in time of war," he said, "there are many ways by which Congress not only has the authority, but is bound to interfere with the institution of slavery in the States........"

---

[1] See *ex parte* Milligan, 4 Wallace, Supreme Court Reports 106. McPherson's Manual for 1867, p. 83 *et seq.*

And on the 14th and 15th of April, 1842, he again reverts to this subject: "I say that military authority takes for the time the place of all municipal institutions, and slavery among the rest, and that, under that state of things, so far from its being true that the States where slavery exists have the exclusive management of the subject, not only the President of the United States, but the commander of the army, has power to order the universal emancipation of the slaves........."

Such was the doctrine recognized and carried into practical effect by the memorable proclamations of September 22, 1862, and of January 1, 1863.

"I, Abraham Lincoln, President of the United States of America, and commander-in-chief of the army and navy thereof, do hereby proclaim and declare........ That on the first day of January, in the year of our Lord one thousand eight hundred and sixty-three, all persons held as slaves within any State or designated part of a State, the people whereof shall then be in rebellion against the United States, shall be then, thenceforward, and forever free........."

He then promised to acknowledge and maintain the freedom of the slaves thus emancipated. And on the first of January, 1863, he published a second proclamation, announcing that from that date slavery was abolished in. the States and districts in insurrection.

This was a most striking application of the principles announced twenty years before by John Quincy Adams. Congress, in the spring of 1862, had doubtless taken some action looking to the abolition of slavery, but that nefarious institution received the fatal blow from the *war power*, which, as some contend, the Constitution holds in reserve for a national crisis. Thus, in somewhat less than eighteen months after the first gun of the rebellion had been fired, he, who March 4th, 1861, scarcely dared to affirm the right of the Union to take measures of defense, was in possession of almost unlimited authority.[1]

But the President did not stop there ; he deduced other consequences from the doctrine relative to the *war power*. Adopting that principle of international law which authorizes the commander-in-chief of an army to set up a provisional administration in conquered districts, he concluded that it devolved upon him to reorganize the seceded States. In his message of December 8th, 1863, he communicated to Congress a copy of a proclamation designed to bring about the return of the Southern States into the Union, and which, after excepting

[1] The reader who may desire to understand how the doctrine relating to the *war power* was developed and carried out, ought to read the speech of Mr. Charles Sumner, delivered in the Senate, May 19, 1862; it was published in pamphlet form, and entitled " Rights of Sovereignty and Rights of War"; and we also recommend the learned work of Mr. William Whiting, called " The War Powers under the Constitution of the United States."

from its benefits certain classes of insurgents, granted a full pardon to every person who had partici-
pated in the rebellion, with a restoration of all
rights of property, except as to slaves, upon condition that such person should take and thereafter
keep inviolate an oath to support and defend the
Constitution of the United States, and to abide by
all the legislation of Congress and the proclamations of the President having reference to slaves.

The proclamation added: "If a number of persons, not less than one-tenth in number of the votes
cast in such State at the presidential election of the
year of our Lord one thousand eight hundred and
sixty, each having taken the oath aforesaid.........
shall re-establish a State government which shall
be republican.........it shall be recognized." It
also recommended to the States which should
adopt this mode of organization, to take the necessary measures to improve the condition of the
freedmen.

Mr. Lincoln's message explained the proposition.
Speaking of the clause that related to the freedmen, he said: "But if it be proper to require, as
a test of admission to the political body, an oath of
allegiance to the Constitution of the United States,
and to the Union under it, why not also to the
laws and proclamations in regard to slavery?
Those laws and proclamations were enacted and
put forth for the purpose of aiding in the suppres-

sion of the rebellion. To now abandon them
would be not only to relinquish a lever of power;
but would also be a cruel and an astounding breach
of faith." And this was followed by the pointed
declaration, " While I remain in my present position
I shall not attempt to retract or modify the emancipation proclamation ; nor shall I return to slavery
any person who is free by the terms of that proclamation or by any of the acts of Congress." This is
not the occasion to inquire into the intrinsic merits
of his plan of reconstruction. It is important, however, to remark that neither the message nor accompanying proclamation evinces the least doubt of
his right to exercise the vast power which he
assumed. Until then, his attempts at reconstruction had been confined to the States or parts of
States which, in his capacity of commander-in-chief,
he administered provisionally as soon as they were
conquered and occupied by the federal troops.
Moreover, at the time when he proposed the general question of reconstruction and communicated
his own views to Congress, it had not as yet resolved upon any definite policy in this respect ; bills
had been introduced, but not discussed ; he had not
then before him any legislative action to serve as a
guide. However, it is evident that he believed
himself authorized to undertake alone this great
work. He held that it belonged to the executive
to proceed to the reorganization of the States, and

that each House of Congress ought to confine itself to respectively examining, at the proper time, the credentials of the Senators and Representatives who might be chosen by the reconstructed States.

Nevertheless Congress at once made known to Mr. Lincoln that they did not concur in his opinion on the division of constitutional powers.[1] The House appointed a special committee, whose duty it was to examine the whole subject of the reorganization of the States, and to report a bill. This step was significant; and the choice of the chairman was particularly so.[2]

The 15th February the committee proposed a bill. An almost interminable debate then followed, so that it was only in the last moments of the session that the two Houses agreed upon its provisions. It was therefore after the adjournment of Congress that the time accorded by the Constitution to the President to enable him to examine all legislative measures presented to him, expired. He availed himself of this circumstance, and did not sign the bill. But he went much further; he addressed a

[1] The proclamation of the President contained this significant sentence: "And for the same reason it may be proper to further say, that whether members sent to Congress from any State shall be admitted to seats constitutionally, rests exclusively with the respective Houses and not to any extent with the executive........" See the message and proclamation in McPherson's "History of the Rebellion," p. 140 *et seq.*

[2] Mr. Henry Winter Davis was at that time one of the determined opponents of Mr. Lincoln.

proclamation to the people on this subject. After having expressed his opinion on the measure, he said that he did not renounce his own plan of reconstruction. This was a grave declaration; it clearly denoted that he did not limit himself to a disapproval of any specific portion or portions of the bill passed by Congress, but that he still claimed the right to reorganize the conquered States. This brought upon him a violent opposition; leading members of Congress protested, in a public address, against what they called "a usurpation of power." The President, said they, attaches no importance to a decision of Congress in the exercise of its constitutional rights; he should, nevertheless, understand that its authority is paramount *and must be respected.*[1]

This occurred in the midst of the presidential campaign. The address had the effect of bringing his decision prominently before the people; they gave him their emphatic approval.

When Congress re-assembled in the following December, Mr. Lincoln insisted upon the immediate admission of the Representatives and Senators chosen by Louisiana. He affirmed that New Orleans and the neighboring parishes had reorganized a republican government in accordance with his plan, and that it only remained for Congress to decide

[1] "The History of the Rebellion," by McPherson, p. 317 *et seq.* A complete account of this important matter will be found there.

whether the Representatives of this State, so re-organized, were entitled to their seats.

The question thus put was debated during the entire session of Congress. However, the tactics of the opposition prevailed; they succeeded in postponing from time to time a final vote, and reaching the 4th of March without any action.

Thus, at the very time that the civil war was on the eve of its termination, Mr. Lincoln energetically maintained his right to dictate to the Southern States the conditions of their return to the Union; while the two Houses of Congress hesitated, and finally adjourned without coming to any decision. The Confederacy collapsed shortly afterward. Some days later he was assassinated, at the very moment when all resistance to the authority of the federal government had ceased. Vice-president Johnson immediately entered upon the office.

History will never know exactly what, during his second term, would have been Mr. Lincoln's policy with regard to the conquered States. Would he have claimed the absolute right to solve, without the aid or concurrence of Congress, the difficulties attending the re-organization of the South, or would he, on the contrary, have compromised with that body? No one can positively say. However that may be, nearly two years later the acknowledged *leader* of the House of Representatives thus treated this much controverted subject: " That

good man," said Mr. Thaddeus Stevens, speaking
of Mr. Lincoln, " who never willingly infringed
upon the rights of any other department of government, expressly accorded to Congress alone the
power to declare ' when or whether members should
be admitted to their seats in Congress from such
States.' It is not to be denied that his anxiety for
the admission of members from Louisiana—or
rather from New Orleans and adjoining parishes—
gave uneasiness to the country. The people had
begun to fear that he was misled, and was about to
fall into error. If he would have fallen into that
course, it is well for his reputation that he did not
live to execute it. From being the most popular,
he would have left office the most unpopular man
that ever occupied the executive chair. But that
over-ruling Providence that so well guided him did
not permit such a calamity to befall him. He
allowed him to acquire a most enviable reputation,
and then, before there was a single spot upon it, ' he
sailed into the fiery sunset.' Here, if there were
anything in common but their station [Mr. Lincoln
and Mr. Johnson], what a temptation to draw a
parallel. But it would be unprofitable ; especially
in this debate. For what we say at the graves of
admired friends, or statesmen, or heroes, is not
biography. The stern pen of history will strip
such eulogies of their meretricious ornaments. But
there is no danger that the highest praise that the

most devoted friends could bestow on him would ever be reversed by posterity. So solid was the material of which his whole character was formed, that the more it is rubbed the brighter it will shine. Mr. Lincoln also was of humble origin (and who is not that is formed of the coarse ' clay of humanity ?') and earned his living by manual labor. But he had too good taste ever to boast of the accident of his birth...........He rose to the Chief Magis-tracy of the great republic by his sterling patriotism, sober habits and modest worth. He was not thrown into power by any moral or political convulsion. His elevation was no accident, but the result of the cool judgment of a nation of freemen. No man ever assumed such vast responsibilities under such difficult circumstances, except, perhaps, William the Silent. How similar in their lives; how alike in death !

"If there was danger, and I admit there was some apprehension that Mr. Lincoln would be beguiled by his chief adviser into a course which would have tarnished his well-earned fame, that good Guardian who had guided him so well, preserved him from that calamity. Death is terrible. Death in high places is still more lamentable ; but every day is showing that there are things more terrible than death. It was better that his posthumous fame should be unspotted, than that he should endure a few more years of trouble on earth. All must regret the manner of his death ; yet, looking to futurity and to his own personal position, it may be considered happy. From the height of his glory he beheld the promised land, and was withdrawn from our sight.........Like the prophet of the Lord, who knew not death, he was wrapt from earth to heaven along a track no less luminous than his who ascended in a chariot of fire with horses of . fire. Would to God that some small portion of the mantle of our Elijah had fallen on his Elisha." [1]

It is certain, from the most positive information, that neither Mr. Johnson nor the members of Mr. Lincoln's cabinet, by whom he was surrounded, had any doubt as to the constitutional power of the President, over the re-organization of the Southern States. Mr. Johnson and his advisers did not then appear to suppose that Congress should intervene in any manner. So he decided not to call an extra session, and entered upon this question at once, and with vigor. The preamble of his proclamation of May 29th, 1865, affirms his full and complete authority in the matter.

" Whereas," says this paper, " the fourth section of the fourth article of the Constitution of the United States declares that the United States shall guarantee to every State in the Union a republican

1 Speech delivered in the House of Representatives, March 19th, 1867, by Mr. Thaddeus Stevens.

form of government, and shall protect each of them against invasion and domestic violence; and whereas, the President of the United States is, by the Constitution, made commander-in-chief of the army and navy, as well as chief civil executive officer of the United States, and is bound by solemn oath to faithfully execute the office of President of the United States, and to take care that the laws be faithfully executed; and whereas, the rebellion ....deprived the people of the State of North Carolina of all civil government; and whereas, it becomes necessary and proper to carry out and enforce the obligations of the United States to the people of North Carolina, in securing them in the enjoyment of a republican form of government." The President consequently appointed a provisional Governor, and charged him to proceed to re-organize the State conformably to the plan traced in that paper. The same system of reconstruction was at once applied to the other States. Thus the Executive Power actually undertook to make a definite disposition of the fate of ten States of the Union.

If the President had accepted the ideas and adopted the policy of the party to whom he owed his position, it is, to say the least, doubtful whether Congress would ever have raised the question as to his constitutional power in the premises. However, he evidently wished to please the Democrats;

not only therefore did he arrogate such power, but some of the leading features of his plan were in con-flict with the cherished principles of the Republican party.

It was then chiefly the politics of Mr. Johnson that provoked the resistance of Congress and led them to assert their exclusive right to decide upon measures of reconstruction. In the month of De-cember, 1865, the reaction commenced; the two Houses were scarcely assembled when they adopted a resolution, which, without expressly contesting his jurisdiction, nevertheless directed a special committee to inquire "Upon the condition of the States that composed the so-called Confederate States of America, and to make a report upon the question as to their right to be represented in the two Houses." Thus Congress was still upon the defensive; it did not declare that he had usurped an authority which exclusively belonged to it. Sev-eral months later the committee on reconstruction went further, and affirmed in its report that he had exceeded the limit of his powers. This memor-able paper, drawn up by a Senator whose recent death has left a wide void in the upper House, maintained that at the time the rebellion ceased the inhabitants of the rebel States were destitute of all civil government. In such a situation it was the duty of the President to cause to be executed all the national laws in those States, and to organize, as far as possible, a provisional administration adapted to their condition. As commander-in-chief of a victorious army, and without departing from the principles of international law, he ought to restore order, defènd property, and protect the people against all violence, foreign or domestic; besides, he was at liberty either to convene Congress or to maintain the existing condition of things until the annual meeting of that body.

The President, in prescribing a mode for the organization of North Carolina, and afterward of the remaining Southern States, palpably transcended his prerogatives. He could not interpose as to the system of government that the citizens of these States might adopt; for according to the Constitution of the United States this power belonged exclusively to Congress, so that his plans of reconstruction could only be considered as provisional.[1]

Congress entirely accepted the conclusions of this report. In this situation the President was obliged to appeal to the people to settle the question pending between the legislative branch of the government and himself. Under the influence of very diverse causes they arrayed themselves on the side of Congress. The electoral campaign of 1866 presents in this respect a very peculiar character. In the history of the dissensions between

[1] Report of the Joint Committee on Reconstruction, p. 8 *et. seq.* It was drawn up by Senator W. P. Fessenden.

the executive and the Houses, these elections furnish the instances in which the people have to the greatest extent decided in favor of the legislative power. Nevertheless we must not consider their decision as a proof that their opinion had undergone an entire change, and that henceforth they would withdraw their special confidence from the Executive Power. Mr. Johnson had personally compromised the position of President of the United States, and the popular distrust of him was the real and only cause of this momentary success of Congress. Thenceforward that body, by its enactments following each other in rapid succession, divested him of the privileges and prerogatives which his predecessor had exercised. The reaction went so far, that before his impeachment he found himself almost powerless, notwithstanding some of these prerogatives were conferred on the executive in express terms by the Constitution.

Thus, within a period of four years, a vigorous executive, wielding formidable powers, came forth from the confusion and anarchy into which the country had been thrown in the beginning of 1861. Under the control of unprecedented circumstances these powers, step by step, attained such proportions that President Lincoln, with a stroke of the pen, broke the fetters of 4,000,000 slaves. Nothing could then longer resist his will; he commands hundreds of thousands of soldiers, and a constantly increasing navy; he holds in his hands a complete system of recruiting, and the people pour without stint their money into the federal treasury. The war continues; the Confederacy begins to give way in the struggle. States one after another are snatched from its grasp, and then he alone undertakes to govern and organize them. Soon after, the entire building put up by the insurgents totters and falls to pieces, and one-third of the Union is subject to his sole control. But power changes hands. His successor is unequal to the task before him. A reaction then speedily begins. At this moment both Houses of Congress enter on the stage; little by little they strip him, not only of all the extraordinary powers received from his predecessor, but proceed so far that Andrew Johnson, President of the United States, is finally impeached by the House and tried by the Senate.

17

CHAPTER XI.

THE 7th January, 1867, the House of Representatives of the 39th Congress adopted a resolution instructing the Judiciary Committee to proceed to inquire into the political conduct of the President of the United States. The 7th of March following, the House of Representatives of the 40th Congress again passed this same resolution, so that the investigation was continued without interruption, notwithstanding the renewal of the House.

The Judiciary Committee heard a considerable number of witnesses, and collected an enormous mass of written testimony, and finally, the succeeding 25th November, made three reports to the House. The first, signed by five Republicans, recommended the *impeachment* of President Johnson; the second, signed by two Republicans, pronounced against the measure, while the third was intended to make known to the House and the country the protest of two Democrats, members

(258)

of the committee. The first two reports merit
special attention. The majority report contained
seventeen articles of impeachment, all, in their
opinion, proved by the testimony before them,
and incriminating the whole political conduct of
Mr. Johnson. The majority reproached him with
grave excesses of power, and believed themselves
capable of establishing his repeated violation of
several laws. It remained to be shown that these
imputed malfeasances constituted an impeachable
offense. And at this point the first question to
determine was the nature and extent of the criminal proceeding known under the name of *impeachment.*

The report of the two dissenting Republicans
said that the Constitution of the United States declares that "the House of Representatives shall
have the sole power of *impeachment.*" What is,
then, the character and scope of this power? May
it be legally exercised at any time that the majority
of the House sees fit to get rid of an obnoxious
functionary? Happily, observes the report, this is
not the case. According to the Constitution, "The
President, Vice-president, and all civil officers of
the United States, shall be removed from office on
impeachment for and conviction of treason, bribery,
or other high crimes and misdemeanors."[1] The
words treason and bribery are easy to interpret.

[1] Constitution, Article II. Section 4.

They describe acts which may be the subject-matter of an indictment before the ordinary criminal tribunals. The law defines them and determines the punishment which may be inflicted on the convicted party. But what is the meaning of the expression, "other high crimes and misdemeanors," employed in the same connection? Do they authorize the House to impeach a functionary in case that his alleged offense would not render him amenable to the courts of criminal jurisdiction?

In inserting the words "treason and bribery," the framers of the Constitution manifested their intention to limit the cases in which the House could exert its power of impeachment. Thus the article referred to has in view only criminal acts, in the ordinary sense of the penal law. And the proof that this interpretation should be given to the Constitution is found in the concluding words, "the party convicted shall nevertheless be liable and subject to indictment, trial, judgment and punishment according to law." Thus the trial by impeachment may terminate by a judgment removing from office and disqualifying the party convicted, but, after such judgment, he is also liable to criminal prosecution in the courts; so that the House cannot proceed by way of *impeachment* unless the accused functionary is charged with a crime or misdemeanor which subjects him to such prosecution. This same report then took up another line of argument, and contended in substance that an impeachment could not be rightfully ordered, unless the alleged act had been made the subject of legislation by the United States. Thus the indispensable conditions to the impeachment of a functionary by the House are

1st. That the act charged should be of a nature to give rise to ulterior criminal proceedings, under the jurisdiction of the courts.

2d. That the crime or misdemeanor is punishable by a law of the United States.

This last point is of great importance, for in a country governed in part by the English common law, and in part by laws enacted by the several States, an offense, provided for only by the common law or a State statute, would not authorize an impeachment. Federal legislation must define the crime or misdemeanor and prescribe the punishment. According to this doctrine, a functionary might be guilty of an offense punishable at common law, but not by act of Congress; but in such a case the House could not impeach him.

These views on the clauses of the Constitution applicable to impeachment were, doubtless, not accepted by a majority of the committee; but the House understood that the minority had received them from an eminent jurist; and it was, moreover, not greatly inclined to push matters to an extremity. So, after a somewhat brief debate, 108 votes were cast against, and 57 in favor of the impeachment.[1]

It thus appears that the House was unwilling to initiate an impeachment solely upon political grounds. The majority thought that the people, as the only judge competent to determine such questions, would, at the following election, decide between the Republican policy of Congress and Mr. Johnson's Democratic tendencies. However, he was soon to change the views of the House on the subject.

As has already been seen, Congress, the 2d March, 1867, passed, over the presidential veto, a law regulating the tenure of civil offices. Section 1st said: "That every person holding any civil office to which he has been appointed by and with the advice and consent of the Senate, or who shall be hereafter appointed to any such office, and shall become duly qualified to act therein, is and shall be entitled to hold such office until his successor shall have been in like manner appointed and duly qualified." This provision signified that any functionary nominated by the President and confirmed by the Senate could not be removed, except in case the Senate should authorize the change by confirming the nomination of a successor. The same section contained a special clause relating to members of the Cabinet. These latter were to hold their offices respectively for and during the term of the President by whom they might have been appointed, and they were only subject to removal by and with the advice and consent of the Senate.

The second section embraced the cases where, during the recess of the Senate, an officer should be shown, by evidence satisfactory to the President, guilty of misconduct in office, or crime, or should become incapable or legally disqualified to discharge its duties. The President could then suspend him and designate a person to perform, temporarily, his duties, but should report to the Senate, within twenty days after the first day of the next session, such suspension, with the reasons therefor. The Senate would proceed to examine them, and if it decided that they were not well founded, the suspended officer was to be reïnstated in his functions.

At the time that the law was debated and passed, the Republican party scarcely concealed their intention of retaining in the War Department Mr. Stanton, who possessed and deserved their entire confidence.

In the course of the summer of 1867, Congress not being in session, the President availed himself of the occasion to ask for the resignation of Mr. Stanton, who answered by a refusal. Mr. Johnson then suspended him, and confided the temporary administration of the War Department to General Grant. Things remained in this condition until the Senate met again in December, 1867. Mr. Johnson then hastened to send a message to that body, setting forth the reasons that had decided him to suspend Mr. Stanton. The 13th January, 1868, the Senate declared that it did not approve them. Consequently, by the terms of the law, Mr. Stanton was to be reïnstated in office. Mr. Johnson appeared at first to yield, and accept the situation; but about a month later (the 21st February) he addressed the following letter to the Secretary of War:

"SIR: By virtue of the power and authority vested in me, as President, by the Constitution and laws of the United States, you are hereby removed from office as Secretary for the Department of War, and your functions as such will terminate upon the receipt of this communication.

"You will transfer to Brevet Major-General Lorenzo Thomas, Adjutant-general of the army, who has this day been authorized and empowered to act as Secretary of War *ad interim*, all records, books, papers and other property belonging to the government, and now in your custody and charge."

As soon as Mr. Stanton received this letter he transmitted it to the House of Representatives. That body referred it immediately to the committee on reconstruction. The selection of this committee foreshadowed coming events; it was almost entirely composed of determined adversaries of the President, and Mr. Thaddeus Stevens, one of the leaders of the Republican party, was its chairman.

The House was not kept long in suspense by this committee. The ninth section of the tenure of office act declared that every violation of its provisions should be considered·a misdemeanor, and it prescribed the penalty of the party guilty thereof. The opponents of Mr. Johnson thought that they had found all the conditions required by the most scrupulous legists for the impeachment of a functionary. The day after the letter was referred to the committee, Mr. Stevens, on their behalf, submitted a report, accompanied by the following resolution : "That Andrew Johnson, President of the United States, be impeached of high crimes and misdemeanors in office." Three days threafter the House adopted this resolution by a vote of 126 to 47, and immediately appointed a committee to prepare and report articles of impeachment. It thus acted because, in its opinion, the President had willfully violated an act of Congress containing a penal provision.

However, when the lawyers composing a portion of the committee examined the question calmly, they perceived how difficult of execution was the work that they had undertaken. So Mr. Thaddeus Stevens, the most discerning and skillful amongst them, suggested the addition of two articles, with a view of bringing the charges, as far as possible, within the limits of a political question. As the House had already voted for the impeachment, it readily consented to accept articles which it had rejected nearly two months ·before. It then appointed managers to present and defend the articles of impeachment at the bar of the Senate.

In the meantime the Senate had formed itself into a high court of justice. Conformably to the Constitution, the Chief Justice of the Supreme Court presided.

Mr. Johnson called upon some of the most eminent jurisconsults of the Union, and they undertook his defense.

The United States then presented an unexampled spectacle in the history of the world: that of a President continuing the administration of affairs, whilst a high court of justice deliberated on his fate. Those who ordered his impeachment, did not dare to suspend him from the exercise of his functions during the trial. And how was the court constituted? Did it not consist of the same Senators who had decided, by a majority of 35 to 6, that Mr. Stanton ought to resume his functions, and who again still more recently had given votes quite as significant? So that the proceedings opened under influences the most unfavorable to the accused.

However, the benignant spirit of the Anglo-Saxon criminal procedure, when conducted even under the most adverse circumstances, was soon felt and recognized. Above all declarations of the rights of man and of the citizen, it guarantees

individual liberty; it does not permit the prosecu-
tor to exhume the entire past of the accused; it
excludes hearsay evidence; it confines the proofs
to the specific charge; it orders that the witnesses
shall be heard in person, and undergo the ordeal of
a cross-examination conducted pursuant to rules
well fitted to elicit the truth; it compels the attendance of witnesses for the defense, and, by the most
solemn sanctions enjoins upon the judges absolute
impartiality. Finally, it forbids the barbarous practice of interrogating the accused, which prevails in
countries where justice is not administered according to the forms of the English common law. Under
such circumstances, there is an equal contest between him and his accusers.

Thanks to the power of that spirit which animates the Anglo-Saxon race, the Senate of the
United States, however hostile to Mr. Johnson, was
governed by these beneficent rules of procedure,
which alone are suited to a free people.

It is impossible to sum up in a few pages the
memorable discussions that commenced the 23d
March, 1868, and terminated the following 31st of
May, by the complete acquittal of Mr. Johnson; the
special study they deserve would far exceed the
space at our command. It will then suffice to show
on what ground this august tribunal decided that it
could not depose him for political reasons.

Among the arguments urged in behalf of the

House, that of Mr. Thaddeus Stevens particularly claims attention. Although in his declining years, and so physically exhausted that he could scarcely take part in the trial, he submitted a paper presenting his views with perfect clearness and precision. Appreciating the difficulty of proving beyond a reasonable doubt that the President had been guilty of a misdemeanor in the dismissal of Mr. Stanton, the manager on the part of the House reasoned as follows: " When Andrew Johnson took upon himself the duties of his high office, he swore to obey the Constitution and take care that the laws be faithfully executed. That, indeed, is and has always been the chief duty of the President of the United States.........to obey the commands of the sovereign power of the nation and to see that others should obey them.........a duty which he could not escape, and any attempt to do so would be in direct violation of his official oath ; in other words, a *misprision of perjury.* I accuse him, in the name of the House of Representatives, of having perpetrated that foul offense against the laws and interests of his country."

Mr. Stevens also accused the President of having willfully usurped the legislative power of the nation in his attempted reörganization of the Southern States, and of having advised them not to submit to the action of Congress. This guilty *animus* was manifest in all his official acts. So the Senate should find in them proof of criminal intention in the removal of Mr. Stanton.[1] He then asked for the conviction of the President, not merely because he had committed a specified misdemeanor, but chiefly because he had resisted the policy of Congress.

But the advocates for the defendant insisted that the Senate was then organized as a distinct body from the Senate acting in its legislative or executive capacity, and was sitting as a court bound by the rules governing criminal prosecutions and securing the rights of the accused. The question at issue was not whether the President had opposed the policy of Congress, and sought to secure the prevalence of his own views in conflict with it, but whether he had committed a crime subjecting him to a subsequent prosecution in a court of the United States. Party considerations should be discarded, and the Senate must confine itself to the judicial determination of the matters involved.

Assuming these positions, which they led the Senate by degrees to accept, the counsel of Mr. Johnson were able to resist successfully the attacks of the managers on the part of the House against the President. At the same time public passions were allaying, and opinions, formed under the influence of violent excitement, gave way to a sober second thought, which commenced considering the question on its intrinsic merits. Finally the court

[1] Proceedings in the trial of Andrew Johnson, p. 665 *et. seq.*

retired to deliberate. During this solemn session it examined, in its turn, the doctrine of the political deposition of the President.

Mr. Sumner gave his unqualified assent to the principles laid down by Mr. Stevens. According to him, the impeachment constituted a political, and not a judicial, procedure. The Senate was not a high court of justice, but it judged as a Senate. He therefore concluded that political offenses might authorize the impeachment and conviction of the party who had committed them. He then retraced the entire public course of Mr. Johnson since his accession to office, and expressed the opinion that it was such as to justify his removal. From this stand-point, the pending proceedings furnished, so to speak, only an occasion for pronouncing his conviction.

He said, in conclusion: " In the judgment which I now deliver I cannot hesitate. To my vision the path is clear as day. Never in history was there a great case more free from all just doubt. If Andrew Johnson is not guilty, then never was a political offender guilty before ; and if his acquittal is taken as a precedent, never can a political offender be found guilty again. The proofs are mountainous. Therefore you are now determining whether impeachment shall continue a beneficent remedy in the Constitution, or be blotted out forever, and the country handed over to the terrible process of revolution as its sole protection. If this milder process cannot be made effective now, when will it ever be? Under what influences? On what proofs? You wait for something. What? Is it usurpation? You have it before you, open, plain, insolent. Is it the abuse of delegated power? That, too, you have in this offender, hardly less broad than the powers he has exercised. Is it the violation of the law? For more than two years he has set your laws at defiance, and when Congress, by a special enactment, strove to restrain him, he broke forth in rebellion against this constitutional authority. Perhaps you ask still for something more. Is it a long catalogue of crimes, where violence and corruption alternate, while loyal men are sacrificed and the rebellion is lifted to its feet? That also is here. The apologists," added the speaker, "are prone to remind the Senate that they are acting under the obligation of an oath. So are the rest of us, even if we do not ostentatiously declare it. By this oath, which is the same for us all, we are sworn to do 'impartial justice.' ....Therefore I cannot allow the quibbles of lawyers on mere questions of form to sway this judgment against justice. Nor can I consent to shut out from view that long list of transgressions explaining and coloring the final act of defiance. ....Something also has been said of the people now watching our proceedings with patriotic solicitude, and it has been proclaimed that they are wrong to intrude their judgment. I do not think so. This is a political proceeding which the people at this moment are as competent to decide as the Senate."[1]

But this opinion, expressed with such force and eloquence, was resisted by another entirely at variance with it. "The power of impeachment," argued one of the most distinguished lawyers in the Senate. "is conferred by the Constitution in terms so general as to occasion great diversity of opinion with regard to the nature of offenses which may be held to constitute crimes or misdemeanors within its intent and meaning. Some contend, and with great force of argument, both upon principle and authority, that only such crimes or misdemeanors are intended as are subject to indictment and punishment as a violation of some known law. Others contend that anything is a crime or misdemeanor, within the meaning of the Constitution, which the appointed judges choose to consider so; and they argue that the provision was left indefinite from the necessity of the case, as offenses of public officers, injurious to the public interest, and for which the offender ought to be removed, cannot be accurately defined beforehand; that the remedy provided is of a political character, and designed for the protection of the public against unfaithful

1 Trial of Andrew Johnson, p. 958 *et seq.*

and corrupt officials. Granting, for the sake of the argument, that this latter construction is the true one, it must be conceded that the power thus conferred might be liable to very great abuse, especially in time of great party excitement, when the passions of the people are inflamed against a perverse and obnoxious public officer. If so, it is a power to be exercised with extreme caution when you once get beyond the line of specific criminal offenses. The tenure of public offices, except those of judges, is so limited in this country, and the ability to change them by popular suffrage so great, that it would seem scarcely worth while to resort to so harsh a remedy, except in extreme cases, and then upon clear and unquestionable grounds.

"In the case of an elective chief magistrate of a great and powerful people, living under a written constitution, there is much more at stake in such a proceeding than the fate of the individual. The office of President is one of the great co-ordinate branches of the government, having its defined powers, branches and duties, as essential to the very framework of the government as any other, and to be touched with as careful a hand. Anything which conduces to weaken its hold upon the respect of the people, to break down the barriers which surround it, to make it the mere sport of temporary majorities, tends to the great injury of

18

274 THE EXECUTIVE POWER

our government, and inflicts a wound upon constitutional liberties.........The removal from office of the chief magistrate should be free from the taint of party ; leave no reasonable ground of suspicion upon the motives of those who inflict the penalty, and address itself to the country and the civilized world as a measure justly called for by the gravity of the crime and the necessity of its punishment. Anything less than this, especially when the offense is not defined by any law, would in my judgment not be justified, by a calm and considerate opinion, as a cause for removal of a President of the United States."

He then proceeded to show that the Senate ought to confine itself to the specific charges preferred against the accused in the articles of impeachment, and to the proofs offered to establish them. He added these memorable words :

" To the suggestion that popular opinion demands the conviction of the President on these charges, I reply that he is not now on trial before the people, but before the Senate. In the words of Lord Eldon, upon the trial of the Queen, 'I take no notice of what is passing out of doors, because I am supposed constitutionally not to be acquainted with it.' And again, 'it is the duty of those on whom a judicial task is imposed to meet reproach and not court popularity.' The people have not heard the evidence as we have heard it. The responsibility is not on them but upon us. They have not taken an oath to 'do impartial justice according to the Constitution and the laws.' I have taken that oath. I cannot render judgment upon their convictions, nor can they transfer to themselves my punishment if I violate my own. And I should consider myself undeserving the confidence of that just and intelligent people who imposed upon me this great responsibility, and unworthy a place among honorable men, if, for any fear of public reprobation, and for the sake of securing popular favor, I should disregard the conviction of my judgment and my conscience.

" The consequences which may follow either from conviction or acquittal are not for me, with my convictions, to consider. The future is in the hands of Him who made and governs the universe, and the fear that He will not govern it wisely and well would not excuse me for a violation of His law."[1]

The Senator who uttered these noble words is no more. May they be meditated on and understood by all those who desire to establish in other countries a free republican government.

These opposing views were presented with equal clearness and ability. The time for a decision had now come. According to the terms of the Consti-

[1] Opinion of William P. Fessenden. Trial of Andrew Johnson, 937 *et seq.*

tution the conviction of the President required a
vote of two-thirds of the Senators present; and it
is due to this protecting clause that Mr. Johnson
was acquitted. [1]

In this way the procedure by way of impeachment, which had been until then undefined, and
which under certain exceptional circumstances
might have menaced the President, was explained,
and a precedent solemnly established which in all
probability will be accepted as binding in all subsequent similar cases.

The result proves how difficult in the future will
be such a proceeding. Unless the evidence adduced
clearly shows that the President has committed a
crime or a misdemeanor, subjecting him to indictment and punishment as for a violation of a federal law, it will be almost impossible to convict
him. He is then independent. Congress ought not
to rely upon an impeachment as a means of con-
trolling him.

It may, without doubt, be said that practically
the President is not liable to any jurisdiction; that
during the exercise of his power he is freed from
the dictation of the people as well as of the legislative authority. But if the people could depose
him, a much more serious inconvenience would
ensue, for he would then cease to be independent.

[1] As will be seen, we do not here express an opinion on the suffi-
ciency of the proofs to sustain the articles of impeachment.

This would bring about an anarchy fatal to the country, and still more fatal to liberty.

If, on the other hand, the Senate had the power to remove a President who did not concur in their opinions, the legislative branch of the government would become supreme, and he be wholly subordinated to it. Then the adjustment of equal powers counter-balancing each other, framed by the convention of 1787, would instantly be destroyed. The United States would be governed by all-powerful assemblies. Would they profit by such a change? Certainly not. In democracies an assembly is generally incapable of directing the government. It may make laws and be peculiarly fitted to restrain power, but is nearly always unsuited for its prolonged exercise.

Thus the fathers of the American republic, having to choose between an imperfect presidential responsibility, and the much greater evils growing out of popular or legislative intervention, evinced great wisdom in assuring the independence of the Executive Power !

CHAPTER XII.

CAUSES WHICH MIGHT MODIFY THE CONSTITUTION OF THE UNITED STATES.

COTEMPORARY documents prove that the framers of the Constitution were not at all assured of its duration; for we seldom find in the journals and writings of the day, an expression of unalloyed satisfaction. The convention limited itself to proposing to the people to make an experiment.

A feeling of doubt and uncertainty continued up to the close of that century. Even after the presidency of Washington many Americans had serious misgivings about the future of the republic. When a new party came into power under President Jefferson[1] prominent Federalists believed that the experiment of a republic had failed.[2] However, Jefferson took a juster view of things. If, as he said in 1796, "an anglican, monarchical, aristocratical party has sprung up, whose avowed

[1] March 4, 1801.

[2] Letter of Jefferson to Philip Mazzeio, 24th April, 1796. See Jefferson's Writings, Vol. IV. p. 193.

object is to draw over us the substance as they have already done the forms of the British government; the main body of our citizens, however, remain true to their republican principles; the whole landed interest is republican, and so is a great mass of talents."[1] After 1801 the republic became consolidated, and assumed those strongly marked features which it has ever since retained. The people have no longer any doubt of its stability, and even begin to think that it is destined to immortality.

It is not our province to contradict them. However, it is proper to note lurking in these institutions the causes of ruin, whose development and growth statesmen should labor to arrest.

The American republic is founded upon universal suffrage. The constituted authorities depend upon the people, the supreme arbiters, who are called upon from time to time to pronounce decisions from which there is no appeal. Hitherto they have performed this duty with remarkable intelligence. It is not then surprising that the great political school, founded by Jefferson, has placed absolute confidence in their wisdom, and, it might almost be said, their infallibility. However, why refrain from here recalling the very different opinion that Hamilton had the courage to express? He says: "It is an unquestionable truth, that the

Jefferson's Writings, Vol. IV. p. 347.

body of the people in every country desire sincerely its prosperity, but it is equally unquestionable that they do not possess the discernment and stability necessary for systematic government." [1]

So far Jefferson, rather than Hamilton, appears to have been right.

However, it must be remarked, that a government was never established upon a principle more logical and at the same time more easy to be perverted. What constant efforts are required to render an entire people capable of mastering the most complex questions of policy and government! What a degree of virtue and wisdom in the masses do such institutions pre-suppose? And, nevertheless, the very day when they lose these rare qualities, the main spring of a republican government will be broken.

If the capacity of the citizens of the Union for self-government, their sense of right and love of public justice deteriorate, the first symptoms of the change will probably be noticed in the organization of the States. It may happen that first at one point, and soon after at another, unrebuked corruption will commence in the local governments. They will then be subject to rapid decay. From the day when they can no longer be maintained in all their original vigor and purity, or become incapable of answering the great ends for which they were created,

the people will naturally look to the federal authority and ask that it may be substituted for them.

The opinions of Hamilton confirm this view.
This determined partisan of a strong central power
strenuously labored to increase the prerogatives
of the President, and to diminish, to the greatest practicable extent, those of the States. His
speech in the convention and the draft which he
submitted furnish conclusive proof of this.[1] He
favored the appointment by the general government
of the executive of each State, who was to be invested with a negative upon its legislation. He
would thus have destroyed in part these local autonomies, and this proposition was in harmony with
the general features of his plan.

Now the continued existence of the American
republic may be largely ascribed to the refusal of
the convention to adopt the views of Hamilton.
Whenever the American people shall reverse that
decision and modify the Executive Power as he
desired to organize it, the inauguration of a new
republic might, perhaps, be possible; but the institutions founded by the convention of 1787 will
have ceased to exist.

And yet, if there were a publicist so bold as to
affirm that the future existence of the States is
beyond the reach of danger, it would only be
necessary to call his attention to very recent events

[1] The Madison Papers, Vol. II., p. 890 *et seq.*

in the South. The doctrine of State rights and State sovereignty, with all its extreme practical consequences, was never in any part of the Union so widely spread as in Virginia, the Carolinas and Georgia. It was the corner-stone of the political faith of the masses. They clung to it with the fervor and unshaken constancy of true believers, and in the late civil war sealed their devotion with their blood. These commonwealths, during the whole struggle, gave proofs of their endurance and tenacity; yet in 1866 it was held in Washington that they had no longer a government, and that the federal authority might engage in the temporary administration of their affairs without having its will resisted or questioned. Who would have said, fifteen years ago, that such things could come to pass? In view of such significant facts, very rash must he be who should venture to affirm that nothing of the sort could take place elsewhere. But without dwelling upon this longer, it is enough to observe that if the vitality of the local governments should diminish, the central power would be thereby proportionately augmented.

Then the question would at once arise whether the legislative or executive branch of the government would take the ascendancy. Now, whatever may be the apparent strength of the first, it does not require a prophet's eye to foresee the ultimate triumph of the second. It may assuredly happen

.that the legislative assemblies might at first make everything yield to them, but let no one believe in their enduring success; they would soon become powerless, and perish by their own blunders. They would believe themselves sustained, long after they had been abandoned by the people, and a day would come when they would be in danger of annihilation without even understanding the reason.

At the time when the American Constitution was formed, political science did not possess that information on the nature of legislative assemblies which experience has since furnished. As we have seen, the convention took every precaution against what was called " the usurping instincts of legislative bodies." It did not calculate the effect of democratic institutions upon public habits and modes of thought, nor, in a society where all are equal, the predilection of the masses for the Executive Power. No one at that time · appeared to suspect that the President might one day become the favorite representative of the people.[1]

1 Jefferson, in his autobiography, has made a remark upon the assemblies of his day which deserves to be quoted. He says: "I served with Géncral Washington in the Legislature of Virginia before the Revolution, and during it with Dr. Franklin in Congress, and I have never heard either of them speak ten minutes at a time, nor to any but the main point, which was to decide the question." Jefferson wrote these lines in 1821, and added: "If the present Congress errs in too much talking, how can it be otherwise in a body to which the people send one hundred and fifty lawyers, whose trade it is to question everything, yield nothing, and talk by the hour? That one hundred and fifty lawyers should do business together, ought not to be expected."—*Jefferson's Works,* *Vol. 1., pp.* 58–59.

However that may be, so long as political activity · in the States remains undiminished, and the existing division of sovereignty between them and the national government continues, the equilibrium between the legislative and the executive authority · will not be deranged. The latter can not imperil the Constitution, unless the local autonomies first disappear or become sensibly weakened.

But these are not the only dangers to which the Constitution may eventually be exposed. We have elsewhere seen in what manner President Washington became the faithful interpreter of the thoughts of the Philadelphia Convention. The Administration he organized proposed to avoid as far as possible foreign complications. As shown in another chapter of this book, he, on retiring from office, insisted upon the continuance of his policy of neutrality. The faithful adherence of his successors to it has essentially contributed to maintain the republic. An active and energetic foreign policy necessarily implies that the executive who directs it is permanent and clothed with powers in proportion to his vigor of action. At the same time, combinations with other governments can be of value only so far as they are upheld by an exhibition of adequate strength, or in other words, they cannot be formed without strongly organized land and sea forces.

If, then, a passion for conquest and territorial

acquisitions should take root and spread in the United States, it would soon and inevitably lead to an increase of the powers of the President. A glance at the map of North America will show that the United States may be extended, either by the annexation of Canada, the conquest of Mexico or the acquisition of the Larger and Smaller Antilles. In their essential characteristics the people of Canada are not unlike those of the republic; almost all speak English, and are accustomed to the working of a free government. Were they to be incorporated into the Union, they would readily conform to its customs and institutions. But such assuredly would not be the case with the Mexicans or the mixed population of different races in the Antilles. Whenever the government acquires these countries, it will be obliged to exercise direct authority over them and provide for their wants; in a word, to establish and maintain, in their midst, a complete organization of the public service. Then it would itself enter upon a new departure, and assume a preponderating importance. The executive would be led to a constant and vigorous intervention in the affairs of the annexed territories. Whenever his sphere of duty becomes thus enlarged, the Constitution will have undergone such vital changes that it will be scarcely recognized. A very strong government will then be developed, much more resembling the favorite plan of Hamilton than that which sprung from the deliberations at Philadelphia.

If, then, the exercise of popular sovereignty such as has been witnessed for more than eighty years, should cease, and the organization of the States lose its present strength, the powers of the central government, and especially the executive branch, would in a corresponding degree be enlarged. It is also quite true that a change of foreign policy and an undue territorial extension would, for different reasons, bring about an analogous transformation. In a word, the political machinery of the United States is so constructed that if any one of its principal pivots or springs be displaced or injured, the whole system would cease to work.

In case the national government, by reason of some one of the causes just indicated, should become greatly extended, would it be possible to establish a responsible ministry to represent the President in the two Houses, and the majority of the two Houses in his council? In other words, could the forms of the constitutional monarchy of England be eventually applied to the republic? An insurmountable objection is at once presented. The President is elected by the people, represents the people, and is only responsible to the people. Were he forced to select a Cabinet subject to parliamentary influences, and virtually constituting the executive government, he would be placed in an anomalous and trying situation. He would cease to be the personal chief whom the American Democracy has been accustomed to respect and the greater part of the time to follow. The reason for his responsibility would no longer exist. The power would then in fact pass into the hands of Congress. Now it is, to say the least, very doubtful if Americans would consent to be governed by a ministry representing the sense of that body and liable to be displaced at its will. They could then no longer recognize, in the direction of public affairs, the individual action of their own elected chief magistrate.

The convention understood thoroughly all the machinery of the British constitution, and generally admired it. Almost all the members did justice to the political institutions of the mother-country; and yet they rejected the idea of a responsible ministry, considering it as incompatible with the republic they wished to found. They thought that the ministry in England was designed to reconcile monarchy and popular representation; that a council having charge of the public interests should be placed between the crown and parliament. But when the United States substituted the elective principle for hereditary royalty, the President was chosen by the people to govern in their name, and he should therefore be responsible only to those from whom he derived his power.

This is so true, that even Hamilton, who pre-

ferred a presidency for life, and would have endowed the incumbent with large prerogatives,
refused to subject him to ministerial control.

But even supposing that the jurisdiction of the
national government should be enlarged, and the
presidential power greatly augmented, it would still
be impossible to organize a parliamentary ministry
without producing confusion and anarchy. This
innovation would speedily displace the center of
the government, and Congress would, for a season,
absorb almost the entire sovereignty; but soon the
democracy, recalled by its instincts, would earnestly
insist for a personal, acting and responsible chief
magistrate.

OPINIONS OF THE PRESS.

[*The Nation.—August* 28*th,* 1873, *page* 147.]

A FRENCH STUDY OF AMERICAN POLITICS. [1]

Having been in this country for several years, during a period of great political activity and excitement, M. de Chambrun has had ample opportunities for observation and enquiry. The spirit of his work is philosophical, and its scope coextensive with an examination of the history, progress and tendencies of American constitutional government. The present volume on the Executive Power is to be followed by three others, one of which is to be devoted to the discussion of the national sovereignty, and what is called in France the "pouvoir constituant," another to the legislative, and another to the judicial power. The present volume will thus apparently be the second of the series.

M. de Chambrun has done his work with care and sense. Taking the "Federalist" for his guide, and supplying himself with current information, both out of his own experience and that of Mr. Sumner, Mr. Schurz and Mr. Caleb Cushing, he has produced a treatise on the executive power of considerable ability. *   *   *

· M. de Chambrun is of the old school, though not entirely of the old school. Indeed, we may say that his study of American politics has brought him to conclusions with

---

(1) Le Pouvoir Exécutif aux Etats-Unis ; Etude de Droit Constitutionnel Par M. Adolphe de Chambrun. Rouse's Point, N. Y. Imprimé ét publié par John Lovell, 1873.

19

regard to practical questions which are in the main dictated by considerations such as would suggest themselves
to an American ; but there is in the speculative part of his
work sometimes a tendency to treat politics as if it were
an exact science, in the mathematical or perhaps rather
mechanical way which would be pursued through a study
of the resultant forces of human.action—each citizen being
considered as a mechanical unit, governed by political
laws corresponding to those of matter. For example, in
discussing centralization, after referring to Hamilton's
plan of a highly centralized government, and comparing
his views on the subject of popular sovereignty with those
of Jefferson, the author says, evidently having in mind
existing political facts, that if the country were moving
toward the pit of centralization, it would probably be in
the local state organization that we •should see the first
indications of it: "It might be that, first at one point, and
then at another, that corruption would insinuate itself in
the local governments; then institutions now vigorous
would be exposed to rapid decay. The day when the people were no longer capable of maintaining them in the
plenitude of their force, they would naturally turn their
eyes to the Federal government; the local governments
having become inadequate to their own needs, would be
driven into demanding of the central power the substitution of itself for them." In this way the ideas of Hamilton
would justify themselves. (p. 349.)   *   *   *

All discussions about such matters as centralization, "co-
ordinate and independent" powers, or the machinery of
representation, lead to little unless they are preceded by
and based upon a study of the actual condition and history
of the society with reference to which they are carried on.
The truth of this proposition M. de Chambrun thoroughly
recognizes, though he at times lapses from its application.
As an illustration of his perception of this fundamental
truth, we may refer to the wise warning he gives French

readers not to be led away into the belief that because a
Republic has worked well in America, therefore, it is suited
to all other countries. He insists on the unquestionable
fact that the men who founded the government were not
aiming at establishing what now goes by the name of "The
Republic." They had the Republic as little in their minds
as they had the Revolution or the Commune. They
desired to arrange a government which would replace the
government they had overthrown, and they based their
new plan on a lifelong empirical study of the country they
meant to govern. *   *   *   *   *   *

The truth was that most of the leading men of the time
were sentimentally attached to the English monarchy, and
with regard to forms of government were probably inclined,
like most veteran politicians and statesmen, to look upon
them with a skeptical eye, and to doubt whether Pope had
not after all been right in allotting to fools discussions
about political forms, and to wise men discussions of practical remedies for evils of administration. It had been the
corrupt and oppressive administration of England, not the
monarchy, for which they had sadly broken with the past.
Another illustration of the same good sense may be found
in M. de Chambrun's mode of treating the proposition to
engraft upon the American system a responsible ministry,
after the English fashion. He points out, as we have often
done in these columns, that a responsible ministry would,
in our system, be utterly incongruous. The English ministry is a Parliamentary Committee which has really
absolute administrative power, though it governs in the
name of the crown. In America, the Executive power
being in the hands of an elective and responsible President,
the circumstances are totally different. The erection of a
responsible ministry would increase the power of Congress,
and at the same time diminish that of the President, and
it would completely upset the balance of power established
by the Constitution. The English system is a gradual

growth of the English constitution, and has no more fitness
for the American Government than the substitution of
French prefects for the governors of States would have.

It is impossible for us to examine in detail all the practical conclusions at which M. de Chambrun arrives in the
course of his examination of the Executive power. His
discussions include such subjects as the election of the
President and Vice President, the constitution of the executive power, the organization of the departments, and the
subordinate official system ; the relations of the President
with Congress ; the right of declaring war (a valuable
chapter) ; the relations of the President with the judiciary ;
the Senate considered as an executive council; the relations of the President with the State; the condition of the
Executive Power under Mr. Lincoln; and the impeachment of Mr. Johnson.

[*From the Philadelphia Press—Extracts.*]

CHAMBRUN ON EXECUTIVE POWER IN THE UNITED STATES.

OBSERVANT Americans have had frequent occasion to
note the difference in character and style between the
writings of Frenchmen on the United States and those of
Englishmen. Examples exist of some few trivial and ill-
tempered French writers concerning us, like Assollant, for
instance, not possessed of wit enough to impart vitality to
their malice. Meanwhile it is difficult to find, among
English travelers here or English writers at home, any
solid and substantial work on the United States.

*   *   *   *   *   *   *   *

We repeat, the works written by Frenchmen on the
United States are of a higher order, and dedicated to the
careful study and candid exhibition of the true character
of society and of government in America. Such is the
spirit of the earliest among the French travelers in the

United States; for instance, the Duc de la Rochefoucald-Liancourt and M. Brissot de Warville, and it is conspicuously apparent in all those of a recent date, such as M. Ampere, M. Duvergier de Hauranne, and above all, M. de Tocqueville, whose great work is indeed a classic essay on the philosophy of government as illustrated in the political history of the United States. And the same spirit animates the writings of Frenchmen at home; as, for instance, the political and historical writings regarding us from the pen of M. Edouard Laboulaye, and of Madame Cornelis de Witt, daughter of M. Guizot, and of M. Guizot himself, the patriarch of the literature and statesmanship of France.

We now have before us another remarkable work on the United States, by a Frenchman, lately published, entitled " Le Pouvoir Exécutif aux Etats Unis, Étude de droit Constitutionnel, par M. Adolphe de Chambrun." M. de Chambrun has resided many years in Washington, with ample opportunity to study the institutions of the United States, not only as they appear on paper, but also in their practical workings as a living fact, and in this work he has discussed those institutions in a spirit worthy of his great predecesᵣ sor, M. de Tocqueville.   *   *   *   *

The work, it is thus perceived, is but the part of a larger design ; that is to say, the exposition of the political institutions of the United States as a whole, the present publication disposing only of so much as relates to the Executive Power. The introductory chapter tends to show that the author may also have had in view the special purpose of enlightening his countrymen on the particular question of how far the republican institutions of the United States are capable of adaptation to France.

*   *   *   *   *   *   *   *

All these important and interesting subjects are discussed by M. de Chambrun on careful consideration of the pertinent political and juridical literature, and with the same acute and discriminating comprehension of the *actualities* of the subject which distinguish the great work of M. de Tocqueville, and which are also perceptible in the instructive work of M. Bagehot on the British constitution.

M. de Chambrun's book is one which every American may read with pleasure, because of the candor and good faith with which it is written, and with profit, because of its complete and acute analysis of our institutions, notwithstanding its more particular application to the great questions of public policy which are now undergoing discussion in France.

[*Extracts from notice of the Baltimore Gazette.*]

WHAT A STRANGER THINKS.

We have had an opportunity of examining a very curious and interesting publication. It is a tract, as it were, a "study" of a single constitutional theme—"Executive power in the United States." It is written in French, the author being M. DE CHAMBRUN, an attaché or counselor of the French Legation at Washington. As the production of an observant and intelligent foreigner, it is very curious indeed. It purports to be one of a series of essays on the Federal Constitution, but is, in itself, perfect and complete, and, beginning literally at the beginning, it shows us what, in the judgment of a stranger, Executive prerogative has grown to be. It is strictly seeing ourselves as others see us. The theory of the book may be easily stated. Assuming the ground that the secret of the decay or decadence of written Constitutions has been in the effort to provide with logical precision for all conceivable contingencies, M. DE CHAMBRUN asserts that the vitality of ours is due to its looseness, its accommodating capacity; and of this he finds a notable illustration in the provisions as to the Executive. Years ago Judge UPSHUR, in his admirable essay in reply to STORY's latitudinarianism, detected this looseness of phrase, but, being a strict constructionist, denounced it as a defect, opening the door to great abuse. The French writer, naturally enough, regards it as a merit and tracing our story from WASHINGTON's Neutrality Proclamation—which was not authorized by any letter of the Constitution—down to Mr. LINCOLN's re-construction experiment, endeavors to show, and in some instances does show, the conservative effect of this very exorbitance. The chapter on the WASHINGTON foreign policy, and especially the difficulty with GENET and revolutionary France, is one of the most interesting portions of this pleasing volume. Reading it, one cannot fail to be impressed by the contrast between the French student's almost reverential tone with reference to our past, and the flippant, iconoclastic style of the Englishman, who periodically "does" our history for New England's leading magazine. The portion of M. DE CHAMBRUN's volume which one reads with most interest is that which relates to Executive power as exercised without resistance by Mr. LINCOLN, and attempted unsuccessfully by his immediate successor.

*   *   *   *   *   *   *   *

The story of the LINCOLN and JOHNSON reconstruction experiments is very cleverly told. Much more is implied than is distinctly stated, as, for instance, when, without the expression of an opinion of his own, M. DE CHAMBRUN quotes at length THADDEUS STEVENS' venomous speech in 1867.

There is on all these questions and subjects a dispassionate and meditative air in this book that is at once winning and impressive. It is a valuable contribution to the political literature of the times, and, as such, from a stranger's open, we are glad to be among the first to welcome it.

[Appleton's Journal.]

AN opportune work at this time of the formation of republican governments in Europe, is that just published by the Marquis Adolphe de Chambrun, " On the Executive

Power in the United States" (*Le Pouvoir Executif aux États-Unis, Etude de Droit Constitutionnel*). So many changes have taken place in American politics since the publication of M. de Tocqueville's celebrated work, that a supplement to it has become indispensable for the proper understanding of the present status of our constitutional law; and M. de Chambrun, having made American institutions the special object of careful investigation, has acquired admirable qualifications for undertaking this task, and acquits himself of it in a very creditable manner, bringing to bear upon his labors a dispassionate and dignified spirit of inquiry, statesmanlike and judicial views, and the most friendly disposition toward the American people. M. de Chambrun abstains from a discussion of the vast ethnological and psychological changes which have revolutionized the social fabric of this country, since from a few million of European settlers, chiefly of the Anglo-Saxon stock, in whom a vigorous moral mettle predominates to a favorable extent over merely personal aims of life, the population has reached nearly forty million, chiefly recruited from Europeans, who abruptly pass here from pauperism to a life of affluence and luxury, and hence are more devoted than the early settlers to exclusively individual interests. To this social revolution, which may account for many of the present phenomena in public life, M. de Chambrun could not possibly advert as within the scope of his researches, which, as the title of the book modestly avers, is confined to an essay on constitutional law, and deals exclusively with political formulæ, laws, and practices. Yet in the narrower scope which he has himself assigned to his researches, he has achieved a great success by throwing light upon many political and constitutional indications and episodes which heretofore were obscure, especially to the European mind, and by examining, with nice discrimination and a religious regard for standard American authorities, the new complexion of public affairs as created by the civil war; the abolition of slavery; the reconstruction of the Southern States; the greater tendency toward centralization; and the proposed substitution of a direct popular vote for electoral colleges in presidential elections; the proposition to extend the presidential term to six years, and to confine each president to one term instead of making him reëligible after four years' tenure of office; the doctrine of neutrality in foreign affairs; the influence of conventions or packed partisan assemblies upon the expression of the popular will, and by many other peculiar circumstances. M. de Chambrun has arranged his work with great tact, so as to make it useful as a book of reference, and as such it cannot but prove of the highest value to statesmen and constitutional lawyers, as well as to students of American institutions, and especially to those embryo republicans in France and Spain who begin to make experiments in that peculiar political structure which, in this country, though only one hundred years old, seems to possess already all the characteristics of advanced age. The work opens with an introduction, and consists of twelve chapters. It is written in a concise and clear style, making it very readable even to those who would perhaps not enjoy, to the same extent, more intricate specimens of the French language. (Published by John Lovell, Rouse's Point, New York, 1873.) ·

[*The World.—Extracts.*]

EXECUTIVE POWER.

LE POUVOIR EXECUTIF AUX ETATS-UNIS—ETUDE DE DROIT CONSTITU-
TIONNEL. Par M. ADOLPHE DE CHAMBRUN. Rouse's Point, N. Y.:
Imprimé et Publié par John Lovell. 1873. 8vo pp,. 359.

There are two prominent thoughts the reading of this exceedingly clever volume suggest which we cannot, on the threshold of criticism, refrain from expressing. How utterly unsound and illusory is the notion—a sort of inher-

itance from our ancestors—that no one can write a scientific
treatise upon constitutions and laws expressed in English
but one who speaks and writes the English language. We
are apt to forget that De Lolme was a Frenchman or Swiss.
Here, too, in M. de Chambrun's volume we have a perfectly
scientific "study" of a single constitutional function of our
government, expressed in the most precise language,
founded on a careful examination of authorities which are
exactly given, and evolving with distinctness the results to
which attentive study has led. It is indeed purely a polit-
ico-philosophical evolution, in which, without effort, the
reader accompanies the writer to his conclusion. The other
suggestion prompted is this : How immeasurably inferior
is what may be termed our subordinate diplomacy—our
secretaries of legation and attachés—to those of other
nations.   *   *   *   *   *   *   *
The author has gone laboriously to study the philosophy, theoretical and practical, of this government, seeking
information everywhere: and the ripened fruit is the beginning and a promise of the best and most scientific essay
on the Constitution that has yet appeared. This, too,
under circumstances of embarrassment and difficulty with
reference to matters at home which were quite sufficient
to disarm any less resolute student.   *   *   *
He tells us in his "advertisement" that this modest
"monograph" on executive power is but one of a series
yet in progress, which will only be complete when it shall
have treated of "national sovereignty" (we quote his exact
words) "and constituent power of the legislative function
and of the judiciary." This, then, is strictly a tentative
publication.   *   *   *   *   *   *
It is by no means easy, within our narrow newspaper
limit, to do justice to M. de Chambrun's "evolution." His
preliminary chapter describes the origin of the growth, one
branch of which he strives to illustrate. He feels the perplexity as every one must, in detecting in revolutionary

revelations the germ of "a republic." "It is," says he,
"singularly difficult to find in the writings of the time a
satisfactory explanation of the manner in which 'a republican form of government' was first adopted in the United
States. A few years before his death, Mr. Jefferson took
pains to prepare a memoir, in which he told the part he
had in the struggle of the thirteen colonies—in the Declaration of Independence, and the events which followed it.
The word 'republic' is not once mentioned in this work." M. de
Chambrun dwells largely on the modes of Presidential
election and its obvious deficiencies, taking what we may
now assume to be the popular view of the failure of the
Electoral College machinery and the misery of party domination through the enginery of national conventions. We
have not room to notice further M. de Chambrun's initiate
chapters, hastening to one (seventh) on what is termed
"Federal Administration," which is capital. He dissents
from Judge Upshur's view, who thought, as with prescience
of to-day, the Constitution defective in that it used terms
with reference to the President which left him at liberty (we
quote exactly) "to neglect his duties and enlarge his
powers." M. de Chambrun sees a merit in this, and reasoning, as he evidently does, from the case of our civil war
experience, perhaps he is right. "Why," says he (184),
"have so many written constitutions, monarchical and
republican, been shipwrecked? Simply because they have
been framed with such logical accuracy that their authors
thought they had provided for all contingencies." We
still doubt over this latitudinarianism, and pass on. The
section of this chapter on Washington's policy of neutrality,
which M. de Chambrun regards as an illustration of the
necessity and advantage of an executive stepping beyond
the lines of prescribed power, is really admirable. We can
but allude to it in passing. Of the same merit is that on
"The Senate considered as an Executive Council," especially with reference to treaties.   *   *   *   *

"The Committee of Foreign Relations," says M. de Chambrun, "has always been composed of eminent Senators, and generally has been presided over by statesmen of the first rank. It is enough to mention the names of John Forsyth and Charles Sumner to show with what jealous care the Senate at critical periods has chosen those to whom functions so important and delicate were to be intrusted. It is under them, and thanks to them, thanks during late years to Charles Sumner, that the Committee has played the first part in the history of the foreign affairs of the Union. In the midst of the crises which the United States have encountered he has contributed to maintain the policy founded by Washington; and if occasionally the executive power has seemed to go too far, the Committee has known how to restrain and check it." (p. 249.)

*   *   *   *   *   *   *   *

In his chapter on the "Relations of the President to the States" we recognize M. de Chambrun, with very slight exceptions, such as in his remarks on conscription, holding to sound inter-Federal-Democratic doctrine. Conscious that we have drifted to the very edge of the limits which confine us, we can do little more than direct the reader's attention to one of the closing chapters—that on "What Executive Power Became Under Mr. Lincoln." It is very well done and full of interest.   *   *   *   *

M. de Chambrun's volume, either in the original or in the translation which we learn is projected, deserves the considerate judgment of all American readers.

[*From The Capital—Extracts.*]

LE POUVOIR EXECUTIF AUX ETATS UNIS—UTUDE DE DROIT CONSTITUTIONNEL. PAR M. ADOLPHE DE CHAMBRUN.

M. de Chambrun has given us a book on constitutional law, as applied to the Executive Power as administered in the United States, which will doubtless be carefully studied and well received in France at this moment, where all questions relative to the organization of the Executive authority are of great import.

Since the remarkable political and philosophical work of M. de Tocqueville, no book has appeared written by a foreigner which so ably treats of the peculiar features of our government, which so clearly discerns where danger impends, or so candidly appreciates the far-reaching statesmanship that laid a foundation broad and deep enough to survive the shocks of nearly a century, and yet at this moment presents to the world an almost unparalleled greatness. It is said that M. de Tocqueville was guided and enlightened in his observations when amongst us by the masterly minds of Judge Story and John Quincy Adams; and in like manner, the Marquis de Chambrun has been assisted in arriving at his very just conclusions by the erudition and the vast attainments of those eminent men, Mr. Caleb Cushing and Mr. Senator Sumner. But the guidance of a mentor does not of itself produce wisdom; and, after all due acknowledgments are made, we must continue to admire the philosophical conclusions of a de Tocqueville and the just perceptions of M. de Chambrun. It is greatly to be regretted that a translation of the work has not appeared simultaneously with the original. Our reading and *thinking* public would appreciate some remarks evincing surprising penetration, a careful study of the philosophy of history, and the acumen of a legal mind applied to the close study of our form of government.

The author very justly observes that in the creation of the republic those institutions were chosen by its founders which best adapted themselves to the national traditions and the public sentiment of the country; *that had it been otherwise* success could not have crowned the effort. This observation seems simple enough, yet it is really very profound. For we constantly fail to appreciate this very fact when we ask to have our institutions indiscriminately applied to other countries. Our politicians often raise a great

hue and cry to have a *republic* declared, the moment any
explosion occurs from out the seething volcano of any one
of the governments of the old world. How inconsequent!
We carry our constitution about the world like a bed of
Procrustes, and attempt to fit to it the effete limbs of all
other nations! This is a sort of Sangrado treatment, which
would doubtless prove fatal to as many *legal constitutions*
and bring about as copious blood-letting as the old quack
ever indulged in. Have we ceased to be a political experiment ourselves? Can we boast of an autonomy so perfect
that we can without empiricism prescribe for all others who
are sick or ill at ease?

Our author very clearly and gravely explains the various
manipulations of political parties, the *modus* by which they
make great men, nominate the leaders, and carry on presidential campaigns. All this is decidedly more instructive
than agreeable for a loyal republican, a lover of "equal
rights," to contemplate. Viewed in this mirror, we behold
our "dear public" dancing like a merry set of manikins to
the skillful wire-pulling of a few daring men.

*   *   *   *   *   *   *   *

The remarks of our author are instructive as regards the
position held by the Vice-President, and the various causes
which would be likely always to produce a change of the
policy of the administration on his accession as first magistrate.

We have also presented a careful analysis of the complex powers confided to the Executive, of the inherent
powers vested as a whole, a synthetic view of the Executive relations toward Congress, as well as toward the Judiciary and the Senate, as co-ordinate; also relatively to the
States, in which the not infrequent struggles between the
executive and the legislative power are explained. He
shows that in these contests the Executive has invariably
triumphed. Even when Andrew Johnson was impeached
there was failure of conviction; and although it seemed for

the moment that the power of the Executive had been lessened, yet it soon became stronger than ever in the succeeding administration of General Grant.

In view of *all the facts* he considers "*the Executive Power is independent.*" As to the *duration* of our institutions, this must depend, of course, upon the virtue of the masses. Whenever demoralization reaches the primal source, we must experience either such an increase of centralized power as to cease to be a republic, or we will be subjected to an irresponsible mob law. According to the exposition of M. de Chambrun the people will rather, in such a deplorable eventuality, incline to support an increase of Executive authority, so as to avoid the greater evil.

There are other nice points which have not escaped the critical investigations of this able jurist, but which want of space forbids us to indicate.

www.ingramcontent.com/pod-product-compliance
Lightning Source LLC
Chambersburg PA
CBHW020241290326
41929CB00045B/1360